MODERN WORLD NATIONS

AFGHANISTAN	ITALY
ARGENTINA	JAMAICA
AUSTRALIA	JAPAN
AUSTRIA	KAZAKHSTAN
BAHRAIN	KENYA
BANGLADESH	KUWAIT
BELGIUM	MEXICO
BERMUDA	THE NETHERLANDS
BOLIVIA	NEW ZEALAND
BOSNIA AND HERZEGOVINA	NICARAGUA
BRAZIL	NIGERIA
CANADA	NORTH KOREA
CHILE	NORWAY
CHINA	PAKISTAN
COLOMBIA	PANAMA
COSTA RICA	PERU
CROATIA	THE PHILIPPINES
CUBA	PORTUGAL
DEMOCRATIC REPUBLIC OF THE CONGO	POLAND
THE DOMINICAN REPUBLIC	PUERTO RICO
EGYPT	RUSSIA
ENGLAND	RWANDA
ETHIOPIA	SAUDI ARABIA
FINLAND	SCOTLAND
FRANCE	SENEGAL
REPUBLIC OF GEORGIA	SOUTH AFRICA
GERMANY	SOUTH KOREA
GHANA	SPAIN
GREECE	SUDAN
GUATEMALA	SWEDEN
HAITI	SYRIA
HONDURAS	TAIWAN
ICELAND	THAILAND
INDIA	TURKEY
INDONESIA	UKRAINE
IRAN	THE UNITED STATES OF AMERICA
IRAQ	UZBEKISTAN
IRELAND	VENEZUELA
ISRAEL	VIETNAM

Belgium

Updated Edition

George Wingfield

Series Editor
Charles F. Gritzner
South Dakota State University

CHELSEA HOUSE
An Infobase Learning Company

Frontispiece: Flag of Belgium
Cover: Colorful buildings in Bruges, Belgium

Belgium, Updated Edition
Copyright © 2012 by Infobase Learning

Chelsea House
An imprint of Infobase Learning
132 West 31st Street
New York NY 10001

The Library of Congress has catalogued the earlier edition as follows:

Wingfield, George.
  Belgium / George Wingfield
     p. cm. — (Modern world nations)
  Includes bibliographical references and index.
  ISBN 978-0-7910-9670-3 (hardcover)
  1. Belgium—Juvenile literature. I. Title. II. Series.

  DH418.W56 2008
  949.3—dc22   2007045818
  ISBN 978-1-61753-044-9

Chelsea House books are available at special discounts when purchased in bulk
quantities for businesses, associations, institutions, or sales promotions. Please call
our Special Sales Department in New York at (212) 967-8800 or (800) 322-8755.

You can find Chelsea House on the World Wide Web at
http://www.infobaselearning.com

Series design by Takeshi Takahashi
Cover design by Jooyoung An
Cover printed by Bang Printing, Brainerd, Minn.
Book printed and bound by Bang Printing, Brainerd, Minn.
Date printed: November 2011

Printed in the United States of America

10 9 8 7 6 5 4 3 2 1

This book is printed on acid-free paper.

All links and Web addresses were checked and verified to be correct at the time of
publication. Because of the dynamic nature of the Web, some addresses and links may
have changed since publication and may no longer be valid.

Table of Contents

Belgium

Updated Edition

1

Welcome to the Kingdom of Belgium

The small country of Belgium hugs the coast of the North Sea in northwestern Europe. It is bordered by Germany to the east, the Netherlands to the north, and France to the south and southwest. The smaller Grand Duchy of Luxembourg borders Belgium's southeast corner. There, the dense forests and rolling hills of both countries constitute a region known as the Ardennes. Less than 70 miles (110 kilometers) to the west, across the narrow Strait of Dover, lies the island of Great Britain. Belgium, the Netherlands, and Luxembourg together form a group of three countries referred to collectively as Benelux. Thus, two small kingdoms and a grand duchy are sandwiched together between the large and powerful republics of Germany and France.

Belgium occupies an area of approximately 11,800 square miles (30,500 square kilometers), making it not much larger than the state of Maryland. With a population of about 10.5 million people, its population density of 884 per square mile (342 per square kilometer) makes Belgium about twice as densely packed as Maryland as well. This density is not far behind that of the Netherlands, which is among the highest in Europe. The country is located at the heart of one of Europe's most highly industrialized and urbanized regions. One consequence of the dense urbanization in Belgium is that its highway network is tightly concentrated. In fact, it appears so brightly lit at night that astronauts orbiting in space can easily see it! The country's capital and largest city is Brussels (French: Bruxelles; Dutch: Brussel). This sprawling urban center has a population of slightly more than 1 million, with more than 2 million people inhabiting the metropolitan area.

Belgium's position on the borders of French-speaking and German-speaking Europe means there is considerable linguistic diversity. More than half of the population (58 percent) are Flemings who live mostly in the northern provinces, in a region known as Flanders. They speak a strongly localized variety of Dutch called Flemish. In the southern regions (Wallonia), the inhabitants, known as Walloons, speak French. The Brussels-Capital region in the center of the country is officially bilingual, but the vast majority of the people speak French, the first language for 40 percent of the country's population. German speakers account for just 1 percent of the population, mostly in the east.

Before 1830, there was no such country as Belgium. This land was then part of the United Kingdom of the Netherlands. During the eighteenth century, the region was ravaged by a succession of wars that resulted in claims of sovereignty by both the royal dynasty of Spain and that of Austria. In addition, parts of the Netherlands and the region that is now Belgium were invaded by the armies of France during the French Revolutionary Wars. Some years later, in 1815, the British and their allies defeated the French under Napoleon in the decisive Battle of Waterloo. Following this event, the Netherlands were united

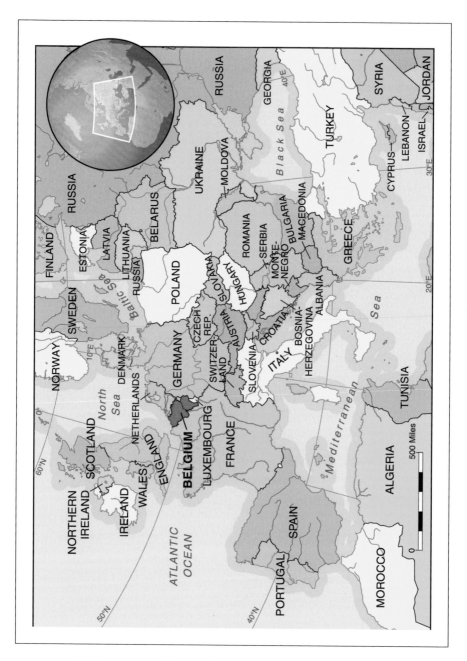

Belgium is one of the smallest and most densely populated countries
in Europe, covering an area of 11,787 square miles (30,528 square
kilometers), which is about the size of Maryland. It is bordered to
the north by the Netherlands and the North Sea, to the east by
Luxembourg and Germany, and to the south and southwest by France.

with the so-called Austrian Netherlands—the land that is now Belgium—by the Congress of Vienna. The Congress, however, failed to take into account conflicting interests and religions. Just 15 years later, the Belgian Revolution of 1830 established an independent, politically neutral, and Roman Catholic Belgium. Thus, the modern country was born.

A government and national congress were established, and Belgium was set on the course of parliamentary democracy. On July 21, 1831, Prince Leopold of Saxe-Coburg was enthroned as king of the Belgians, a constitutional monarch. King Leopold I of Belgium, as he became, was considered a popular choice and a symbol of Belgian nationhood. Since then, July 21 has been celebrated as Belgium's National Day. The monarchy has continued to the present day, and, in 1993, King Albert II became head of state and sixth king of the Belgians.

Belgium was one of the founding members of the European Union (EU) during the second half of the twentieth century. Brussels, as the headquarters of most EU offices and activities, is effectively the unofficial capital of Europe. The European Parliament building and several other EU institutions are situated in Brussels. Brussels hosts the headquarters of the North Atlantic Treaty Organization (NATO), of which Belgium and the United States are both members. The city also hosts several other international organizations as well.

The challenge for the European Parliament today is to reconcile the many national interests and national differences of EU members. It is essential that this be accomplished by democratic and peaceful means, rather than by the bloodshed and warfare that beset Europe during the previous thousand years. This is no small task. As the number of EU member nations increases, more and more national interests must be considered and respected while simultaneously catering to the needs of Europe as a whole.

Following World War II, Belgium joined NATO and, together with the Netherlands and Luxembourg, formed the

Benelux group of countries. It became a founding member of the European Coal and Steel Community in 1951. In March 1957, all three Benelux countries, together with France, West Germany, and Italy, came together to form the European Community (EC)—initially known as the European Economic Community (EEC)—with the signing of the Treaty of Rome. This later expanded to include other nations, such as the United Kingdom, and it was renamed the European Union in 1993. This movement toward a united and possibly even federal Europe has been the political direction of these European institutions for many years, and Belgium has played a leading role. In view of the terrible bloodshed and destruction that afflicted this small country for so many years, one could not dispute that unity, peace, and partnership in Europe was the only sensible way forward.

Despite the cosmopolitan flavor of Brussels and its modern and forward-looking institutions, the Belgians are proud of their heritage and of their fine cities and traditions. This quickly becomes evident to foreign visitors to Brussels and Bruges (Dutch: Brugge), the capital of West Flanders, both of which are popular tourist destinations. At the heart of Brussels is the Grand-Place (Dutch: Grote Markt), a stunning historic square that is the focal point of the city's social and civic life. Lined with ornate guildhalls built mostly in the seventeenth century and home to the great Gothic Hôtel de Ville (City Hall), this square was designated a World Heritage Site by the United Nations Educational, Scientific and Cultural Organization (UNESCO) in 1998. This is where the people of Brussels gather for important ceremonies and festivals. It is also where people come to sit and have a beer and watch the world go by. If you are hungry, you can find restaurants here that serve, among many other dishes, oysters and mussels. Brussels is renowned for its marine delicacies.

A different exhilaration for the taste buds is Belgian chocolate, for which Bruges in West Flanders is deservedly famous.

Grand-Place, or Grote Markt, is one of Brussels's most popular attractions. Wooden houses surrounded the square until the fourteenth century, when affluent residents built stone mansions. It became an important commercial and political center where meetings were held, executions took place, and where royalty were officially received. In 1998, Grand-Place was named a UNESCO World Heritage Site.

Its citizens must be connoisseurs of fine chocolate, for Bruges seems to have a chocolate shop on every corner. There is a seemingly endless supply of handmade chocolates of every imaginable flavor to be found. Here again, the principal city square is the medieval Market Square (Dutch: Grote Markt), with its great 288 foot (83 meter) high Belfry Tower (Belfort) that dates from 1300. Like other belfry towers in Belgian cities, this one houses a sweet-sounding carillon of 47 bells. A weekly market was held in Bruges from A.D. 985 until August 1983— almost 1,000 years—and the late medieval architecture around the square rivals that of Brussels.

Since the sixteenth century, Bruges has been a thriving center of trade and commerce. During the seventeenth and eighteenth centuries, it was a major center for the lace-making industry. Although it might be hard to comprehend today, this trade brought Bruges huge prosperity. Architecturally, the city has changed little since that time, and its canals and a fortified encircling moat give it a unique character that makes it one of the finest historic destinations in Europe. Everywhere in this city, one sees the steep stepped gables of the old houses that are so characteristic of the ancient town buildings in Belgium.

Apart from the Belgian kings and political figures that have shaped this modern country as well as the European Union, one might ask, "Can you name a famous Belgian?" Actually, there are quite a few, as we shall see in a later chapter; however, most people are generally at a loss to name them. Instead, rather curiously, they have sometimes suggested two fictional Belgians whose names are evidently known worldwide: Tintin and Hercule Poirot.

The Adventures of Tintin (French: *Les Aventures de Tintin*) was a series of Belgian comic books created by Belgian artist Georges Remi (1907–1983), who wrote under the pen name Hergé (or Hervé). The series first appeared in French in a children's supplement to a Belgian newspaper in 1929. Set in a carefully researched world that closely reflects our own, *The Adventures of Tintin* presented a cast of characters in distinctive settings and continued to be a favorite of both readers and critics for more than 70 years. The comic strip hero, Tintin, was a young Belgian reporter and traveler. He was accompanied in all of his adventures by his faithful dog, Snowy. Later, popular additions to the cast included Captain Haddock, Professor Calculus, and two bumbling detectives called Thomson and Thompson. To commemorate Hergé's fictional national hero, a giant plastic figure of Tintin stands on one of the buildings in Brussels.

The other fictional Belgian who is a universal favorite is author Agatha Christie's character Hercule Poirot, a private detective with magnificent waxed mustaches. In the tradition of Sherlock Holmes, Poirot is portrayed as a brilliant but eccentric sleuth who invariably solves each crime by his powers of deduction and without much help from his assistant or the policeman assigned to the case. Movies and TV series about Hercule Poirot's exploits have been popular for many years.

We will return to the subject of famous Belgians in a later chapter, but let us finish this one with mention of two nonfictional Belgians who changed the world, each in his own rather different and special way. Adolphe Sax, a musician born at Dinant in Wallonia, invented and patented the instrument that bears his name, the saxophone (invented in 1840; patented in 1846). This musical instrument is quite simply unique, and the rest—as anyone who likes jazz and blues will tell you—is history.

Father Georges Lemaître, a scientist and Roman Catholic priest from Charleroi, was first to propose the big bang theory of the origin of the universe in 1927. He drew conclusions from his own calculations that even Einstein was hesitant to infer. That same year, Lemaître talked with Einstein in Brussels. Einstein, unimpressed, told him, "Your calculations are correct, but your grasp of physics is abominable." However, this was one occasion when Einstein was later forced to eat his words. Today, Lemaître's big bang theory, although somewhat modified, is accepted by scientists as the way in which our universe came into being.

In this book, you will learn about the physical, historical, and human geography of this small but fascinating country and its people. You will travel through its unique natural and cultural landscapes as you come to better know the country's land and people. Enjoy your trip!

2

Physical Landscapes

B elgium has a land area of 11,787 square miles (30,528 square kilometers), which, as already has been noted, is roughly equivalent in size to Maryland. Most of the country's territory lies on a huge lowland plain that stretches from the Pyrenees eastward to the Urals. In this chapter, we will look at Belgium's land areas, its weather and climate, and finally at some of the country's more important environmental pressures and concerns. You also will see how Belgians have adapted to and used their natural landscapes.

LAND AREAS

In terms of land areas, Belgium can be divided into three main geographical regions. These include the coastal plain in the northwest; the central plateau, in which Brussels and the Belgian heartland are situated; and the high plateau of the Ardennes in the southeast.

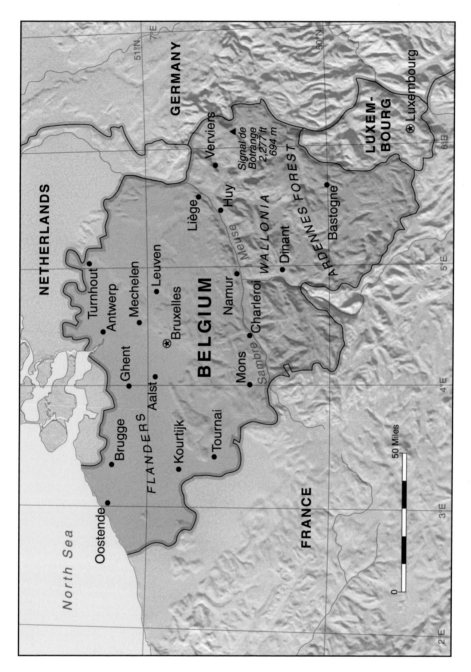

Belgium has three main geographic regions: the coastal plain in the northwest, the slightly elevated central plateau, and the densely wooded, rocky plateau called the Ardennes highlands that extends across southeastern Belgium and into northeastern France. Botrange, the highest peak in Belgium, has an elevation of 2,277 feet (694 meters).

Coastal Plain

The short Belgian coastline is similar to the coast of the Netherlands. It features long, sandy beaches backed by sand dunes that broaden out to the southwest, where the coast reaches the border with France. Behind the dunes are low-lying polders (sections of land reclaimed from the sea and protected by dikes) about 10 miles (16 kilometers) wide. Once covered by marshlands, this land was drained, as it was in the Netherlands. The polders were developed between the thirteenth and fifteenth centuries. This coastal region is bounded by the River Scheldt (Dutch: Schelde), which flows northeast, roughly parallel to the coast, until it empties into the sea near the port of Antwerp and the Netherlands border.

The province of West Flanders largely comprises this coastal region and, further inland from the coast, the plain of Flanders is drained by the River Scheldt and its tributaries. The capital city of West Flanders is Bruges. Ostend (Dutch: Oostende) and Zeebrugge are two major ports on the coast to the west and north of Bruges, respectively. Adjoining this province to the east is East Flanders. Its capital is Ghent (Dutch: Gent; French: Gand; formerly "Gaunt" in English), which is located about 25 miles (40 kilometers) from Bruges. Ghent is situated on the River Scheldt at its confluence with the Lys, approximately 30 miles (50 kilometers) west of Brussels.

During the Middle Ages, Ghent became one of the largest and richest cities of northern Europe, with some 65,000 people living within its protective walls. Until the thirteenth century, it was the second biggest city in Europe (after Paris)—larger even than London. Today, it is a busy city that includes a port and a university. The city is connected to the sea by the Ghent-Terneuzen Canal. Much of Ghent's medieval architecture is still intact and is remarkably well preserved and restored. The city center is the largest car-free zone in Belgium. The city also hosts the annual Ghent Festival, a 10-day street festival that attracted 1.5 million people in 2007.

The late sixteenth and seventeenth centuries brought devastation to the city as a result of religious wars. At one time, Ghent was a Calvinistic republic, but the Spanish army eventually reinstated Catholicism there. These wars ended Ghent's role as a center of international importance. A curious fact is that the War of 1812, fought between the United States and Great Britain, was ended by the Treaty of Ghent. This document was signed by diplomats from both countries who met in the city in 1814. Unaware of the peace treaty, the commander of the U.S. forces, Andrew Jackson, moved his soldiers to New Orleans, Louisiana, at the end of 1814. There, he decisively defeated the British at the Battle of New Orleans. This was hailed as a great victory, making him a national hero and propelling him to the presidency. Yet it is also a reminder of how slow communications were 200 years ago.

The Central Plateau

The central plateau of Belgium is a primarily smooth region with rolling hills and fertile valleys that are irrigated by rivers, canals, and dikes. Some higher land also exists here, with occasional wooded areas and some gorges and caves. Besides West Flanders and East Flanders, northern Belgium, which is generally referred to simply as Flanders, has three further provinces situated on the central plateau away from the coast. These are Antwerp, Limburg, and Brabant, which is now divided into Flemish Brabant and Walloon Brabant. In the center of Brabant province is the Brussels-Capital region, which surrounds and includes the city of Brussels.

Antwerp (Dutch: Antwerpen, French: Anvers), besides being a great port, is Belgium's second largest city; its population reached 461,500 in 2006. The city is situated on the right bank (as one faces downstream) of the estuary of the River Scheldt that flows into the North Sea. It is also the capital of Antwerp province, which lies mostly to the east of the city. The province's northern boundary is the border with the Netherlands. Terrain here is very similar to that found in the southern Netherlands. It is crossed by many canals, such as the Albert Canal and other waterways.

Antwerp has long been a very important city and a commercial center from both an economic and a cultural standpoint. Its seaport is one of the world's largest; after Rotterdam (in the Netherlands), it is the second largest port in Europe. A high volume of oil refinery traffic in tanker vessels and a large number of cargo ships pass through the port of Antwerp. The city is also considered to be the center of diamond trading, an industry that traditionally has been controlled by families from its large Hasidic Jewish community.

The town square (Grote Markt) is the focal point of this thriving city. Not as big as the Grand-Place in Brussels but certainly as beautiful, it is surrounded by the Town Hall and the old houses of the guilds or corporations. Behind these historic structures, the tower of Our Lady's Cathedral completes this impressive urban panorama. The houses of the guilds are unfortunately not the original ones. A large part of the Grote Markt burned down in 1576. Most of the houses were later rebuilt in the Flemish Renaissance style.

The municipality of Duffel near Antwerp is the origin of duffle (or duffel) coats and bags. The winter coats were made of thick wool and featured hoods and wooden toggle fastenings.

To the east of Antwerp province is Limburg province, whose capital is Hasselt. This province is also quite similar to the Netherlands, which borders it to the north and east, and it too is bisected by the Albert Canal. The part of the Netherlands just east of here is also, confusingly, known as Limburg and contains the city of Maastricht. The great River Meuse (Dutch: Maas) flows north out of Belgium into the Netherlands and forms the border between Belgian Limburg and Dutch Limburg for about 25 miles (40 kilometers).

On the Meuse River in the town of Dinant sits the Collegiate Church of Notre-Dame, built in 1100. Overlooking the church is the eleventh-century citadel, which is reachable by cable car or by walking up the 408 steps cut into the hillside. Adolphe Sax, the inventor of the saxophone, was born in Dinant in 1814.

The old province of Brabant lies at the center of Belgium but is now divided three ways. Flemish Brabant was created in 1995 by splitting the former province of Brabant into three parts: two new provinces, Flemish Brabant and Walloon

Brabant, and the Brussels-Capital region, which (rather like Washington, D.C.) is no longer considered part of any province. This split was made to recognize the official division of Belgium into three separate regions: Flanders, Wallonia, and the Brussels-Capital region. The capital of Flemish Brabant is Leuven, and the capital of Walloon Brabant is Wavre.

Besides Walloon Brabant, French-speaking Wallonia, which effectively comprises the whole southern part of the country, has four further provinces. These are Hainaut, Namur, and Liège, all considered to be in the central geographical region, and Luxembourg province in the Ardennes.

Hainaut (usually spelled Hainault in English) is the most western province of Wallonia and lies to the south of West Flanders and East Flanders and also of Walloon Brabant. Its capital city is Mons, and the province also includes the industrial city of Charleroi, which is either Belgium's third or fourth largest depending on the definition of its boundaries. Geographically, this part of the country is very similar to the rest of the central plateau.

Namur province is sandwiched between Hainaut and Luxembourg provinces in the south central part of Belgium. Parts of the province are quite hilly but not as much as the Ardennes region, which lies to the south. Its capital, Namur, is situated at the confluence of the Meuse and Sambre rivers.

Liège province is the most eastern part of Belgium and lies north of Luxembourg province as well as the Grand Duchy of Luxembourg. The River Meuse flows northeast across the province, and its capital, Liège (Dutch: Luik), is situated on the river. Liège is the third largest city in Belgium after Brussels and Antwerp, although Charleroi also claims the distinction, which, as we have said, depends on where one draws the city boundaries. In any case, Liège is the principal economic and cultural center of Wallonia.

At the beginning of World War I, the Battle of Liège followed the invasion of neutral Belgium by the Germans. It lasted

Liège is the third largest city in Belgium. Once the center for steel production and manufacturing, Liège is now an educational hub, with about 40,000 students attending more than 24 schools. It is also a strong economic center for a variety of industries including space technology, mechanical industries, information technology, biotechnology, and the production of water, beer, and chocolate.

for 12 days and resulted in surprisingly heavy losses for the invaders at the hands of the outnumbered Belgians. This was the first land battle of that war.

During World War II, the Allies liberated Liège from the Nazis in September 1944. Subsequently, it was subjected to intense aerial bombardment; more than 1,500 V-1 and V-2 missiles landed in the city between its liberation and the end of the war. After the war, Liège suffered from the collapse of its steel industry, which produced high levels of unemployment and led to much poverty and social tension.

Again, most of Liège province is part of Belgium's central plateau and includes mainly agricultural land in broad, flat river valleys. The eastern part of the province, which borders Germany, is hillier. This is the district in which Belgium's small German-speaking minority lives.

In this province, 22 miles (35 kilometers) southeast of the city of Liège is the town of Spa. This town is situated in an attractive valley in the hills of the Ardennes, and it is where hot springs, which are claimed to have healing properties, are found. Spa has been frequented as a place to "take the waters" since the fourteenth century. The town has given its name to any resort that has mineral springs with supposed health-giving properties. Taken further, the generic term *spa* is now used to refer to any resort hotel with hydrotherapy facilities, or it can merely mean a hot tub. These days, the town of Spa is equally well known as the location of the racing car circuit for the Formula One (F1) Belgian Grand Prix. The Circuit de Spa-Francorchamps was built for Grand Prix motor racing in 1921 and is one of the most challenging courses in the F1 calendar. The course is famous for its unpredictable weather. At one point in its history, it rained during the Belgian Grand Prix for 20 years in a row.

The Ardennes

Luxembourg province in southeastern Wallonia is principally a wooded plateau in the Ardennes, ranging from about 1,600 to 2,300 feet (500 to 700 meters) in elevation. It lies to the east and south of the River Meuse. The plateau is divided by rivers that flow in places through deep ravines and below craggy bluffs. Agriculture and cattle farming are chief occupations in this rural region. There is some heathland, and peat bogs are found in depressions in the landscape. The highest point in Belgium is the Signal de Botrange, which is only 2,277 feet (694 meters) above sea level, here in the mountains of the Ardennes.

Luxembourg is the largest Belgian province but the most sparsely populated in a densely populated country. The provincial capital is Arlon. Tourism in this area is economically important; in recent years, many farmhouses and other buildings have been converted to provide tourist accommodations. Much of Belgium's remaining wildlife is found in this region.

The Belgian province of Luxembourg lies immediately west of the bordering Grand Duchy of Luxembourg, which is an independent country little more than half its area. The identical name of these two separate geographic entities is confusing, and it is important to distinguish between them. The Ardennes plateau includes most of the northern part of the Grand Duchy of Luxembourg and also extends into France. To the southwest of the Belgian province of Luxembourg is the French Department of Ardennes.

WEATHER AND CLIMATE

Belgium has a temperate climate that is kept mild through the influence of the North Atlantic drift, a warm ocean current that extends northeast from the Gulf Stream. Prevailing westerly winds blow overland from the direction of the English Channel. They bring changeable weather in from the sea, and rainfall can be frequent and sometimes heavy. Winters are usually mild and wet; at this time of year, mists and fog are common. Summers are generally quite cool and pleasant. Greater extremes of both cold and heat are mostly associated with atmospheric high-pressure systems that occasionally move in from the north and east.

In the part of the Ardennes located farthest inland from the coast, more rain and snow falls—due principally to the higher elevation of the land. It is in these uplands that the larger forests are found, and these contain conifers together with oaks, beeches, and other deciduous trees.

Over time, half of the country has been cleared for agriculture or pastureland. In fact, in Europe, only Denmark has more of its area well suited to agricultural pursuits. Besides the forests of the Ardennes, there is also heathland, and this is found especially in eastern areas such as the province of Liège.

ENVIRONMENTAL PRESSURES AND CONCERNS

The environment in Belgium is exposed to considerable pressure from human activities. These primarily include urbanization, industry, a dense transportation network, and extensive farming that involve crop cultivation and animal raising. The consequent air and water pollution certainly have repercussions for neighboring countries. Uncertainties about federal and regional responsibilities for control of this pollution have slowed progress in tackling environmental issues like these. Today, however, most of these matters have been resolved.

From the environmental concerns of modern mankind in present-day Belgium, we can look back to prehistoric times, when early man first lived in this part of Europe. The oldest primitive stone instruments found in the area of today's Belgium date from 800,000 B.C. Between 350,000 B.C. and 40,000 B.C., remains indicate that Neanderthal man was living on the banks of the Meuse River. In caves at the village of Spy, near Namur, nearly perfect skeletons of such early hominids were discovered in 1886. From about 40,000 B.C. onward, *Homo sapiens* supplanted the Neanderthals as inhabitants of the region.

In Wallonia, near the point at which the borders of the provinces Namur, Liège, and Luxembourg meet, is the beautiful village of Wéris. Nearby stands the massive sentinel rock known as La Pierre Haina. This natural monolith in the hills of the Ardennes was evidently a sacred place in prehistoric times. Today, it continues to be venerated by the local people who whitewash the rock in an annual ceremony. The countryside around Wéris is a fascinating prehistoric site that features a field of megalithic remains more than 5 miles (8 kilometers) long. Here, ancient standing stones and dolmens (chamber tombs) over 5,000 years old form an alignment that is unique in Belgium. Traditionally these *champs sacrés* (sacred fields) belong to the early Danubian culture, remains of which have been found buried near the city of Liège to the north. Neolithic megaliths like these are certainly the earliest remains of human-built structures in the region preceding historic times. In the next chapter, we shall consider the history of this land which eventually became modern Belgium.

3

Belgium Through Time

T he area of Europe that includes Belgium lies open and exposed on the European plain. It has often been referred to as the "Battlefield of Europe." Bloody and seemingly endless wars between different European powers were repeatedly fought here. It was not always a single nation known as Belgium; the country's name derived from that of the tribes that inhabited these parts 2,000 years ago. In the first century B.C., the region was conquered by Imperial Rome, and the mostly Celtic tribes, the Belgae, were subdued by the Roman legions. This is the derivation of the name Belgium. During the time of the Roman Empire, it constituted the most northern part of the province Gaul and was known as Gallia Belgica.

After the fall of the Roman Empire, the Franks dominated this region and what is now the Netherlands. This Germanic tribe from the Rhine region controlled the area for several hundred years during the early Middle Ages. These invaders settled mostly in the north, and it was here that their Franconian dialect became the basis of the Dutch language. This replaced Latin as the region's mother tongue, although Latin developed into French, which was spoken in the regions farther south. This influx of Franks was the initial cause of the linguistic split that is so evident in present-day Belgium.

The kingdom of the Franks was called the Carolingian Empire after Charles the Great, who is more widely recognized by his French name, Charlemagne. He was king from A.D. 768 until his death in A.D. 814 and became, during his reign, the powerful ruler of a mighty empire. In his *Short History of the World*, H.G.Wells said: "Charlemagne, who began to reign in 768, found himself lord of a realm so large that he could think of reviving the title of Latin Emperor. He conquered North Italy and made himself master of Rome."

Charlemagne expanded his Frankish kingdoms by conquest into a Frankish Empire that incorporated much of Western and Central Europe. His capital was at Aachen (French: Aix-la-Chapelle), which is now in Germany, just a few miles across the present-day Belgium border from its eastern province of Liège. However, a little over 100 years later, control of the territory that is today's Belgium was divided between the rulers of France and Germany. Most of the Dutch-speaking north came under the influence of France, and the French-speaking south was ruled by the German Holy Roman Empire.

DOMINANCE BY OTHER EUROPEAN POWERS

During the latter part of the fourteenth century, the lands that are now the Netherlands and Belgium—the Low Countries—fell into the hands of the powerful dukes of Burgundy. This meant that they were to become caught up in the long struggle between England and France known as the Hundred Years' War (1337–1453). The bone of contention that led to this lengthy conflict was the claim by English kings to the French throne. The British rulers also repeatedly attempted to regain those lost lands in Normandy that were once part of their Norman heritage.

The last feudal Duke of Burgundy, Charles the Bold (also known as Charles the Rash, or Charles the Terrible) died in 1477 at the Battle of Nancy. With his death, dominion over the Low Countries passed to the Holy Roman emperors, the Austrian Habsburgs. This came about because Charles's sole inheritor was his 19-year-old unmarried daughter, Mary. Both the king of France, Louis, and the Holy Roman Emperor had unmarried elder sons, and they both sought Mary's hand in marriage. The prize was considerable, and the outcome would have enormous implications for the balance of political power. It was a pivotal moment for Europe. In the end, Mary married the future Maximilian I, Holy Roman Emperor, and the Habsburg dynasty became heirs to the Low Countries. In 1504, their son, Philip the Handsome, received the crown of Spain, thereby forging a link between Austria, Spain, and the Low Countries.

During the sixteenth century, this part of Europe was known as the Spanish Netherlands. Dominion over it was soon to be disputed, however, by the Austrian Habsburg dynasty and the Spanish royal dynasty—both considered the Netherlands their possession. However, the Protestant leader William of Orange, also known as William the Silent, hoped to gain independence for the Netherlands. The southern provinces remained loyal to Spanish rule and to Roman Catholicism. In 1579, however, the Protestant north proclaimed the Union of Utrecht, forming the independent United Provinces of the Netherlands under William's leadership. The independent United Provinces initially included Flanders and Brabant, but these were later reconquered by Spanish troops. The Dutch revolt against Spain, which had been lead by William, continued as the Eighty Years' War (1568 to 1648) long after his assassination by the Catholic Frenchman Balthasar Gérard in 1584. The Spanish Netherlands later lost additional territory during the Thirty Years' War (1618 to 1648). In 1700, when Charles II of Spain—last of the Spanish Habsburgs—died, the remaining provinces fell into French hands. French control, however, would not last long, because the Austrians and the English were not going to allow it.

During the War of the Spanish Succession which started in 1701, this land was fought over constantly. The main antagonists were the armies of the English, with their Dutch and Austrian allies, and the armies of the French, who were allied to Spain. The English commander, the Duke of Marlborough, won famous victories at Ramillies (on the border of Namur and Brabant provinces), Oudenarde (in Flanders), and Malplaquet (southwest of Mons). The latter battle, the bloodiest of the eighteenth century, was a costly victory for the English and their allies, who lost 25,000 soldiers—twice as many as the French. Ultimately, many thousands of soldiers died before France's military power was subdued. The war was ended by the Treaty of Utrecht in 1713, although neither the peace nor the balance of power would last. Austrian sovereignty was restored in what had been the Spanish Netherlands in 1748.

Under Austria's Habsburg empress Maria Theresa, this region prospered with the modernization of agriculture and the development of new industry. Many new roads and canals were built. Then, in 1792, just three years after the French Revolution, war broke out between revolutionary France and Austria. Within two years, the French had defeated the Austrians and annexed the Austrian Netherlands.

WATERLOO AND BELGIAN INDEPENDENCE

By the end of the eighteenth century, the Low Countries, comprising the Netherlands and the Austrian Netherlands (which corresponds roughly to present-day Belgium), had been overrun by France during the Napoleonic Wars. This brought the changing dominion of either Austria or Spain to an end. Eventually, a British-led coalition of forces opposed to

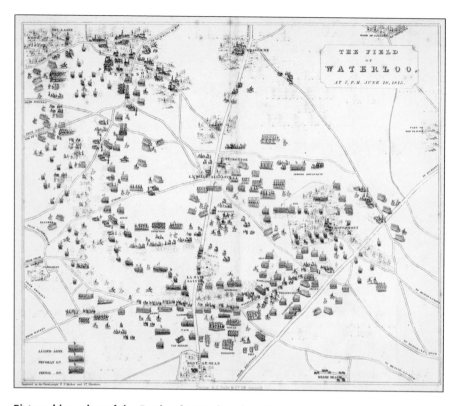

Pictured is a plan of the Battle of Waterloo, fought on June 18, 1815. This final battle in the series of wars between France and several European nations called the Napoleonic Wars brought about the defeat of Napoleon Bonaparte. Peace finally came to embattled Europe for nearly 50 years, until the unifications of Germany and Italy in the last half of the nineteenth century. Napoleon's downfall was so complete that *Waterloo* became synonymous with a crushing defeat.

the French emperor Napoleon confronted his army in 1815. Where would this battle be fought? The answer, of course, was in Belgium—or at least in that unfortunate country that was shortly to become Belgium and seemed always destined to be the battlefield of Europe. The great battle took place at Waterloo, a small village located 7½ miles (12 kilometers) south of Brussels on June 18, 1815. The British and their Prussian allies defeated the French, despite their lesser numbers. Napoleon suffered 25,000 dead and injured and 8,000 soldiers captured; this was the end of Napoleon's rule, and it broke the power of the French Empire.

When Napoleon had been forced into exile a year earlier, representatives of the major European powers had met to redraw the Continent's political map. At the Congress of Vienna, it was decided that the Low Countries would be unified as the United Kingdom of the Netherlands. Plans for this were agreed on despite Napoleon's return from exile and resumption of power. Yet his final "Hundred Days" as emperor were ended by his loss at the Battle of Waterloo and his permanent exile to the remote island of St. Helena, located in the South Atlantic Ocean.

The two regions of the new United Kingdom of the Netherlands unfortunately had conflicting interests, and this was to lead to its dissolution. Just 15 years later, the Belgian Revolution of 1830 established an independent, neutral, and Catholic Belgium, and the modern country came into being. This mutiny against Dutch control, led by the French-speaking upper class, initially aimed to attach the southern part of the Netherlands to France. However, it was prevented from achieving this objective by the great powers of Europe at the time, and the alternative was an independent state. From the early twentieth century onward, French was the dominant language in Brussels as a result of Walloon immigration and enforced gallicization by means of social pressure.

A government and national congress were established, and Belgium was set on the course of parliamentary democracy. In 1831, Prince Leopold of Saxe-Coburg (in Bavaria) was chosen and enthroned as King Leopold I of Belgium, a constitutional monarch. The fact that a figure such as Leopold was crowned king soon after the Belgian Revolution should come as no surprise to those who regard monarchy as the antithesis of democracy. In nineteenth-century Europe, a country would undoubtedly expect to have a monarch as head of state. If it did not have one, it would be natural to seek out a suitable candidate. Such a figure was meant to represent national unity and act as a safeguard against the excesses of revolutionaries and dictators like Napoleon.

WORLD WAR I IN BELGIUM

A hundred years after the Battle of Waterloo, Belgium was once more the battleground for yet another European war of frightening dimensions, which resulted in the slaughter of millions. This was World War I (1914–1918), in which the principal combatants were Great Britain, allied with France, and the German Empire of Kaiser Wilhelm, allied with Austria-Hungary. Toward the end of this war, the United States sent troops to Europe to fight alongside their British and French allies.

In July 1914, Germany invaded neighboring Luxembourg and demanded passage for its troops through Belgium. When this was refused, the Germans at once invaded Belgium and immediately occupied much of the country. In response, the armies of France and Britain joined the battle with the German forces in northern France and Flanders. Many of the bloodiest battles were fought on Belgian soil.

During the early stages of the conflict, the fiercest fighting was around the Belgian town of Ypres (Dutch: Ieper), in West Flanders. In trench warfare, under the ceaseless shelling by enemy artillery, thousands of soldiers on both sides were killed day after day, with little ground being gained or lost. Conditions in the trenches were terrible, and the whole battlefield was often a sea of mud. The fearful carnage of this type of warfare meant that the chances of survival for any soldier who fought in the frontline trenches for any length of time were very small.

It was at Ypres in 1915 that the German forces first used poison gas (chlorine) against the Allies. Two years later, again near Ypres, they introduced mustard gas (which was also known as *yperite,* after the city). The fighting continued for much of 1917 around Ypres, and the battle resulted in nearly half a million casualties on all sides. Yet only several miles of ground had been won by the Allied forces. The town itself was all but obliterated by artillery fire. In Ypres today, the massive Menin Gate Memorial commemorates all of the soldiers from Britain and the British Commonwealth who died in the fierce battles in this part of Flanders and who have no known grave.

Equally horrific were the World War I battles that raged near the Belgian city of Mons (in Hainaut province) and at Passchendale, with similar enormous losses of life. A short distance across the border, in northern France, a quarter of a million soldiers and civilians died at Verdun. The Battle of the Somme, fought in northern France in the summer and fall of 1916, was one of the largest battles of World War I. There were more than one million casualties, and this was certainly one of the bloodiest battles in human history. All of this fighting continued for four years and resulted in an estimated 19 million deaths (half of which were civilians) and another 21 million wounded.

World War I ended with the defeat of Germany in 1918, but the world would never be the same. Millions lay dead, and many towns in Belgium, especially Flanders, and northern France lay in ruins. Peace was established by the Treaty of Versailles in 1919, but its provisions and the punitive reparations imposed on Germany by the Allies failed to address the underlying problems. This should have been the war to end all wars, but it was not. Approximately 20 years later, in May 1940, Germany invaded Belgium once more during the early stages of World War II.

OCCUPATION OF BELGIUM IN WORLD WAR II

Between 1940 and 1944, Belgium, like the Netherlands and most of France, suffered Nazi occupation. It was not until August 1944 that the country was liberated by British and American forces. In 1940 King Leopold III signed an

Resistance groups, also called "the underground," demonstrated many acts of bravery during World War II. On April 19, 1943, three members of the Belgian resistance movement ambushed a Nazi deportation train transporting Jewish and gypsy civilians to Auschwitz. Many prisoners were able to escape. Here, Belgian resistance fighters pose on a captured German tank in Antwerp.

armistice with the invading Germans and opted to stay in Belgium. Most civil servants and police remained in their jobs, but the Belgian government of the day fled to Britain. As in other European countries, the Nazi occupiers rounded up and deported many Belgian Jews. It is estimated that about 25,000 of them were taken to Auschwitz and other concentration camps in Germany and Poland where they were murdered. There have been charges that the Belgian authorities at the time were complicit in these arrests, but they have never been made accountable. This question lingers, however, and a parliamentary report in 2007 entitled "Submissive Belgium" concluded that wartime officials had indeed been guilty. Prior to their deportation, most of the Jewish victims were interned in a transit camp at Breendonk, near Mechelen, where a national memorial now stands.

Because the German occupiers considered Dutch a Germanic language, they enacted laws to protect and encourage the Dutch language in Flanders. Generally, they did what they could to encourage ill feelings between Flemings and French-speaking Walloons. In some cases, they liberated Flemish prisoners but not French-speaking ones. Although the Nazis had no intention of allowing the creation of a Greater Netherlands or a Flemish state, many Flemish nationalists embraced collaboration, believing it would promote their cause.

In 1944, at the end of the occupation, Belgian resistance fighters prevented the Germans from destroying the port of Antwerp. The facility served as a vital base for the continuing Allied advance across Europe. Antwerp was one of the war's most fought-over and highly prized targets due to its deep-water port facilities and the fact that almost all French ports remained in German hands until the very end of the war. After the Nazi forces withdrew from the city, they rained down on it thousands of V-1 and V-2 missiles from launch sites farther inland. These destroyed large sections of the city but, remarkably, not the port.

Even so, the German armies fought a determined rearguard action in the Ardennes region during the Battle of the Bulge. American forces fighting under General George S. Patton and his commander in chief, General Dwight D. Eisenhower, eventually repulsed this attack, but not before the loss of at least 81,000 U.S. troops. This heavy fighting on Belgian soil lasted well into 1945.

During the fighting, the legendary Easy Company of the 506th Parachute Infantry Regiment, U.S. 101st Airborne Division, was one of the units that was cut off and besieged in the town of Bastogne. It was vital that the town not fall to the Germans. Because all seven main highways through the Ardennes converged in Bastogne, Nazi troops would be able to cut off many of the Allied forces to the north and retake the port of Antwerp if it fell. Following heavy losses and much heroism by the Americans, the town was relieved by units of General Patton's Third Army and the wounded were evacuated. These wartime events in Belgium were reenacted in the 2001 HBO miniseries, *Band of Brothers*.

Located in Bastogne is a major U.S. war memorial that honors those men who fell in the Battle of the Bulge. It is one of many such memorials in different parts of Belgium that commemorates the soldiers of different nations who fell in World War I and World War II. Visitors to these monuments can only hope that Belgium will never again be the bloody battleground that it was for so many centuries.

The Yser Tower (Dutch: IJzertoren) is a memorial that stands beside the Yser River in Diksmuide, West Flanders. Two IJzertorens have existed, the first of which was built after World War I by former Flemish soldiers. In March 1946, the tower was illegally demolished by explosives, but the perpetrators were never caught. There were some indications of involvement by the Belgian military and former resistance fighters in the repressive atmosphere that followed World War II. Several years later, a new tower was built on the same location. This tower is the highest peace monument in Europe (275 feet, or 84 meters) and bears the plaintive demand "No More War" in the four languages of the First World War combatants—English, French, Dutch, and German.

As a result of his unpopularity following the war, King Leopold III abdicated in 1951 in favor of his son Baudouin I. Leopold's unpopularity was mainly due to his decision to surrender to Nazi Germany in 1940, when Belgium was invaded. Many Belgians questioned his loyalties, even though a commission of inquiry after the war found him not guilty of treason. A referendum on his continued rule was held. Although he narrowly won this vote, strikes and unrest over the issue nonetheless led to his decision to abdicate the throne.

BELGIUM AS AN AFRICAN COLONIAL POWER

Besides the problems of the monarchy, Belgium's postwar renaissance led to many other political changes. Among these was the future of Belgium's colonial possessions in Africa. For more than 50 years, Belgium was a major colonial power. Its principal colony was the Belgian Congo, which is now known as the Democratic Republic of Congo. In terms of area, this is the third largest country on the African continent, and it is a land rich in natural resources.

Before taking over the Congo as a colony in 1908, the Belgian Parliament had no jurisdiction over the territory that was owned as a private dominion by Leopold II, the second Belgian king. He had sponsored expeditions by European explorers in the territory, the first of which was lead by Sir Henry Morton Stanley. The Congo was formally acquired by the king at the Conference of Berlin in 1885, where his profession of humanitarian objectives was generally accepted because he was then chairman of the Association Internationale Africaine. He made the territory his private property and named it the Congo Free State.

King Leopold's regime began various ambitious projects, including the railroad that ran from the coast to the capital, Léopoldville (now Kinshasa). This took years to complete. Most of his projects were aimed at the fullest exploitation of the colony for financial gain, which resulted in appalling treatment of the Congolese who made up the labor force. In this so-called "Free State," the local population was brutalized by overseers in pursuit of profit to be made from growing and producing rubber from rubber trees. This period coincided with the development of rubber tires in Europe and America, and the rubber trade made a fortune for King Leopold. Using the profits from rubber, he had stately buildings constructed in Brussels and Ostend to honor both himself and Belgium.

During the brutal period between 1885 and 1908, an estimated 5 to 10 million Congolese died as a result of the king's ruthless exploitation. The country's population was reduced by about 50 percent. To enforce rubber quotas, the Force Publique militia was used by Congo's administration to terrorize the local population. This it often did by cutting off the limbs of the uncooperative natives. Such actions provoked widespread international protests and condemnation by well-known figures, such as Mark Twain in the United States.

Leopold gave up his personal property, the Congo Free State, as a result of international outrage over the brutality that took place during his tenure. Its annexation to Belgium was accomplished by means of the treaty of November 15, 1908, which was approved by the initially reluctant Belgian Parliament in August and by the king in October of the following year. Bowing to international pressure, chiefly from Great Britain, the Belgian government agreed to take over this private possession of the king, at which point it became the Belgian Congo.

In addition to the Congo, Belgium also governed the colony of Ruanda-Urundi beginning in 1916. The independent kingdoms of Rwanda and Burundi (formerly Ruanda-Urundi) were annexed by Germany, along with other states in central Africa, in the late nineteenth and early twentieth centuries.

In 1916, forces from the Belgian Congo conquered this area. After the First World War ended in 1918, German East Africa was divided among several European powers by the Treaty of Versailles. The largest area, Tanganyika (today's Tanzania), went to England. Belgium, however, received the much smaller westernmost part of the region that came to be known as the Belgian Occupied East African Territories. In 1924, the League of Nations gave Belgium complete control over the area, which became Ruanda-Urundi.

INDEPENDENCE FOR BELGIUM'S AFRICAN COLONIES

During World War II, the largest known reserves of uranium ore were those in Katanga (one of the provinces of the Belgian Congo). The Belgian company Union Minière du Haut Katanga provided the United States with the uranium that was required for the Manhattan Project in Los Alamos. This was the top-secret project that was carried out to develop the world's first atomic bombs. These were subsequently used in the bombings of Hiroshima and Nagasaki in 1945, which resulted in Japan's surrender and the end of World War II. During the Cold War, the U.S. government continued to purchase uranium from the Belgian company. Extensive use of this resource was made to build America's huge nuclear arsenal. The fact that the main supply of uranium was from the Belgian Congo may well have played a significant part in the political events there during the 1960s. After the Congo was granted independence, both the United States and the Soviet Union politically competed to gain the favor of the country's leaders.

In the 1950s, an independence movement arose in the Belgian Congo, as it did in many other African states that were European-administered colonies. The emerging nationalist movements put Belgium under increasing pressure to transform the Belgian Congo into a self-governing state. In 1960, the country was granted independence from Belgium, and the first self-governing Congolese parliament was inaugurated. King Baudouin personally attended the festivities and gave a speech that was widely considered insensitive to the atrocities that had been committed in the Congo during the reign of his royal ancestor, Leopold II. This speech received a blistering response by Congolese Prime Minister Patrice Lumumba, and political unrest, insurrection, and attempts to secede by various provinces followed. A coup against Lumumba and secession of the mineral-rich Congo province of Katanga occurred soon after independence was achieved. Within seven months of coming

President Mobutu of the Congo *(second from right)* and his family are received as guests by the Belgian King Badouin and the queen in 1968. Later, a treaty of friendship was signed during the king's 1970 visit to the Congo, but diplomatic relations continued to break down over various issues. In 1971 Mobutu renamed the country Zaire, but this name was dropped after Mobutu's fall in 1997.

to power, Lumumba was deposed and assassinated in Katanga, allegedly with Belgian involvement.

The country's postindependence name was the Republic of the Congo until August 1964, when its name was changed to Democratic Republic of the Congo (to distinguish it from the neighboring Republic of the Congo, whose capital is Brazzaville). In 1971, then-president Joseph Mobutu renamed the country Zaire. Following the First Congo War, which led to the overthrow of Mobutu in 1997, the country was renamed Democratic Republic of the Congo. Since 1998, the country has suffered greatly from the devastating Second Congo War, said to be the world's deadliest conflict since World War II.

In 1962, Ruanda-Urundi was granted independence by Belgium as two separate states, Rwanda and Burundi. In these countries, independence was also followed by large-scale ethnic conflict. In this case, conflict existed between the Tutsis and the Hutus, which led to the infamous Rwanda genocide of 1994. This was the mass killing of hundreds of thousands of ethnic Tutsis and moderate Hutu sympathizers in Rwanda, the largest atrocity of the Rwandan Civil War. This genocide was mostly carried out by extremist Hutu militia groups, such as the Interahamwe.

In 1994, Belgian Prime Minister Jean-Luc Dehaene ordered the unilateral withdrawal of Belgian troops from Rwanda, thus lifting the last barrier to this genocide. To most observers, the deadly consequences of his action could easily be foreseen. During questions from a Belgian parliamentary commission into the decision, however, the prime minister repeatedly stated that he had no regrets about his decision. At least 500,000 Tutsis and thousands of moderate Hutus died in the genocide, with some estimates putting the total death toll between 800,000 and 1,000,000.

NATO AND BELGIUM'S ROLE DURING THE COLD WAR

Belgium's history after World War II is not complete without mention of the part it played in the confrontation with the Soviet Union during the Cold War years. Belgium became the host country for several international organizations that played a vital role in the defense of Europe.

On April 4, 1949, 12 nations from Western Europe and North America signed the North Atlantic Treaty in Washington, D.C. A key feature of this treaty is Article 5, in which the signatory members agreed "[an] armed attack against one or more of them in Europe or North America shall be considered an attack against them all." The first Supreme Allied Commander Europe (SACEUR) was the popular and respected U.S. Army General Dwight D. Eisenhower, who led Allied forces in

Europe during World War II. He was appointed in 1950 and immediately set up his Supreme Headquarters Allied Powers Europe (SHAPE) command in Paris, France.

The treaty members had been galvanized into action by the Korean War (1950 to 1953). The world political scene was soon dominated by the Cold War standoff between the United States, with its European allies, and the Soviets who were allied with Communist China. The North Atlantic Treaty would not, however, continue in its original form; France claimed that it served U.S. interests at the expense of French and European ones. France therefore opted out of the alliance and asked U.S. forces and the command headquarters of the treaty to withdraw from its soil.

This break came about when President Charles de Gaulle announced France's withdrawal from the North Atlantic Treaty Organization's (NATO's) integrated military structure in 1966. In 1967 the headquarters of NATO and SHAPE were removed from Paris and reestablished in Belgium. NATO administrative buildings were built in Brussels, and SHAPE headquarters were constructed at Mons. The Belgian authorities had decided that SHAPE should be located at least 30 miles (50 kilometers) from Brussels, NATO's new location, because SHAPE was a major wartime military target. One very visible piece of long-term infrastructure is the SHAPE Bunker, which was begun in 1980 and completed in 1985. SHAPE's most important work during this period was associated with nuclear arms control and improved nuclear plans and procedures. It is in some ways ironic that this nuclear warfare command center was built near Mons. The new location placed it squarely amid the old battlefields of World War I, where so many had perished in the trenches 70 years before.

Despite deep-seated fears of nuclear warfare during the Cold War era, NATO and SHAPE have helped to maintain peace in Western Europe up to the present day. Belgium has remained a NATO member and a staunch ally of the United

States, although its government did not support the U.S.-led invasion of Iraq in 2003. While the threat of nuclear warfare has receded since the breakup of the Soviet Union and the end of the Cold War between 1989 and 1991, we must hope that there will indeed be "No More War." This part of Europe, which was for so long a bloody battleground, may at last be allowed to live in peace and prosperity.

CHAPTER

4

People
and Culture

ew countries are so equally divided by language and other
aspects of culture as Belgium. Yet, despite the conflicting
interests of the two main population groups, the country has
achieved a unity that does not appear to be seriously threatened.
Although there have been, and still are, significant separatist and
nationalist movements, especially among the Flemings, the likelihood
that Belgium will split in two, at least in the immediate future, is slim.
The way of counteracting this nationalism has increasingly been to
introduce greater federalism for the country as a whole.

There is indeed a belief that all the talk of separatism and the
division of the country into independent parts is just that—talk.
The Belgian people appear to like one another and to relish their
nationhood. That, for the majority of Belgians, is more important
than being a Fleming or a Walloon. It is, many will say, just the

politicians who squabble endlessly and play with separatist fire. Separatism is still a minority viewpoint, however, even in Flanders.

During the months that passed after the 2007 general election in Belgium and the failure of the politicians to form a government, there were many quiet displays of national unity. Belgian flags appeared all over Brussels, and one could often see the black, gold, and red tricolors hanging from windows and wrought-iron balconies. Although some flags are seen at national festivals, nothing like this had happened since the time of the late King Baudouin's death in 1993.

This recent display seemed intended as a rebuke to Belgian politicians and a message that they should form a new government. Other patriotic signs were also in evidence. A substantial crowd turned out to march in a parade that commemorated the martyrs of the Belgian independence movement. This is an annual parade organized by a small monarchist group, Pro Belgica. In addition to the usual old-timers—men with formidable mustaches carrying flags and fierce old ladies with Belgian tricolor rosettes—there were many younger people in the march. All were keen to see an end to the political crisis and a return to normality and national unity.

CHARACTERISTICS OF THE POPULATION

Belgium is home to about 10.5 million people, an estimated 10,423,493 in mid-2010. The population is growing at a slow 0.08 percent annually. Deaths (10.5/1,000) exceed births (10.1/1,000) each year. The fertility rate—the number of children to which the average woman will give birth during her lifetime—is 1.65, well below the replacement level of 2.1. Therefore, Belgium's small annual population gain is the result of immigration, which is about 1.2/1,000. This amounts to approximately 10,000 immigrants entering the country each year.

As is true throughout most of Europe, Belgium has an aging population. Life expectancy is slightly more than 79 years,

Belgium, like many European countries, is concerned about the threat to its welfare system due to an aging population. The International Monetary Fund has predicted that by the year 2050 the number of Belgium's elderly will increase by more than 63 percent to over one-fourth of the country's overall population. The government warns that taxes from a shrinking workforce will be insufficient to pay for the growing number of elderly.

82.7 for women and 76.2 for males. Only 16 percent of the population is under 14 years of age, whereas 17.8 percent of Belgians are 65 or older. The median age of 42 years ranks Belgium's population (along with several other European countries) among the world's oldest. An aging population imposes a number of problems upon a country's social structure and economy. Providing for the needs of an aging population, including retirement programs and increased medical care, places an added burden on the country's economy. Fewer people are available to take entry-level jobs, a condition most often solved by increased immigration. Health care surpasses education as a national priority. These are just some of the population-related issues that Belgium, along with most other European states, faces in the near future.

LANGUAGE AND ETHNICITY

As we have already seen, more than half of the 10.5 million people of Belgium are Flemings who speak Dutch or, more correctly, Flemish. These 58 percent live principally in the north, and most of the rest are French-speaking Walloons (40 percent) who live in the southern and eastern provinces. Small numbers of German speakers live in the eastern districts of Liège province. The Brussels-Capital region, comprising about a million people, is 85 to 90 percent French speaking. Certainly French, rather than Flemish, is the language that the majority of immigrants tend to speak when they first come to Belgium.

In the year 2000, the country's foreign residents constituted 8.8 percent of the total population, a number believed to be somewhat higher in 2010. This figure does not include foreigners who reside illegally in Belgium or Belgians of foreign origin who gained Belgian nationality through various means. About 63 percent of these foreigners come from EU countries, and the other 37 percent are from countries outside the EU. These figures from the National Institute for Statistics (2000) also show an uneven distribution of foreigners by region. The greatest proportion of foreign residents (28.5 percent) lives in the Brussels-Capital region, whereas only 4.9 percent of the population in Flanders is foreign. The figure in Wallonia is 10.0 percent.

The foreign population in Flanders is particularly concentrated in the provinces of Limburg and Antwerp. In Wallonia, it is mainly concentrated in the old industrial provinces of Liège and Hainaut. Italians, who total about 200,000 people, are the most numerous of the legal foreign residents in Belgium. Moroccans are the second-largest group, with around 121,000 people mostly concentrated in Brussels. The French, a population that is often ignored in studies on immigration, are in third position, with over 107,000 people. They are followed by the Dutch, with more than 85,000 residents. Turks are in fifth place, with more than 69,000 people. The Spanish number more than 45,000, the Germans more than 34,000, and the British about 26,000. Americans and Congolese (i.e., those from what was previously the Belgian Congo, or later Zaire now known as the Democratic Republic of the Congo) number nearly 12,000 each. Contrary to what many believe, a majority of foreigners living in Belgium are originally from either a member state of the European Union or from other developed Western countries. The immigrant nationals from Africa and some Asian countries are still a minority, even if their concentration in the large urban centers gives them a certain visibility.

RELIGION

The great majority of Belgians are Roman Catholics (about 75 percent), but there is also a small Protestant minority, mostly in Wallonia. A 2006 inquiry in Flanders, long considered more religious than either the Brussels or Walloon regions of Belgium, showed that 55 percent of its inhabitants considered themselves religious. Additionally, 36 percent of those polled in this inquiry claimed to believe that God created the world. Roman Catholicism is traditionally seen as Belgium's majority religion. By 2004, however, weekly Sunday church attendance was reported to have dropped to between 4 and 8 percent of membership. Yet many people who almost never attend Mass still have their children baptized in a Roman Catholic Church.

Another religion practiced in Belgium is Islam (3.5 percent), which is principally the result of immigration by Muslims. There are also small minorities of Protestants, Orthodox, Anglicans, and Jews (each of them constituting less than 1 percent). Belgian law officially recognizes those denominations,

Pope John Paul II visited Belgium twice during his reign. King
Baudouin (*right*) was a deeply religious Catholic, and his spiritual life
supported him in his governmental duties. Upon the king's death in
1993, Pope John Paul II recognized him as "an exemplary king and a
fervent Christian."

as well as certain secular organizations that are organized in the same way as religions. Buddhists have also applied for legal recognition.

Historically, religion was one of the causes of the Belgian Revolution of 1830 and the declaration of an independent Belgian state. Following the defeat of the French at Waterloo, the United Kingdom of the Netherlands split apart to form Belgium and what is now the Netherlands. This was mainly due to the differences between the Roman Catholic south, which became Belgium, and the largely Protestant Dutch in the north.

Since 1830, Roman Catholicism has played a very significant role in Belgian politics. An example of this was the "school wars." This ideological conflict took place from 1879 to 1884, and later from 1954 to 1958, between the political parties that were philosophically to the left (at first Liberals, and later Liberals and Socialists) and Catholics. These "wars" were a result of defiance of Catholic authority in matters that related to education in Belgium.

Another controversy occurred in 1990 when Baudouin, the Roman Catholic and deeply religious king of the Belgians, refused to sign and officially ratify an abortion bill that had already been approved by parliament. Prime Minister Wilfried Martens was asked by the king to find a constitutional solution. Martens achieved this by having Baudouin declared unfit to fulfill his constitutional duties as a monarch for some days, while government ministers signed in his place.

FAMOUS BELGIANS

In this brief chapter about the Belgian people and what makes this country so distinctive culturally, we should not ignore one of the most inspirational aspects of its national heritage. That is Belgium's fine art and the magnificent collection of paintings and other treasures that are to be found in its many museums and galleries. Much of this art was produced well before modern Belgium came into being in 1830. Many of the earlier Renaissance paintings were sacred art inspired by religious themes, but there is much more as well.

One the country's greatest artists was undoubtedly Pieter Brueghel the Elder (c. 1525–1569). He was a Flemish/Dutch Renaissance painter known for his striking landscapes and peasant themes. Although there was no such country as Belgium in his day, Belgium can safely claim him because he was accepted as a master in the painters' guild of Antwerp. He traveled to Italy soon after, and then returned to Antwerp before settling in Brussels permanently 10 years later. He died there in 1569. The subjects of his paintings include meals, festivals, dances, feasts, and games. Certainly he paid extraordinary attention to detail, showing a vivid tapestry of life in those times. Some of his works can be found in the Musée des Beaux-Arts in Brussels.

An earlier Flemish artist who can also be claimed by Belgium is Jan van Eyck (1385–1441), one of the greatest painters of the late Middle Ages. He was once held to have been the inventor of oil painting, but the fact is that he developed new and highly successful techniques in this medium, with magnificent results. One such masterpiece is his *Arnolfini Portrait,* which shows the merchant Arnolfini and his bride. This work, which is full of religious symbolism, has been analyzed again and again by art historians. The painting has become something of a cult image, rather like Grant Wood's *American Gothic* has in the United States. It was painted in 1434 in Bruges, where van Eyck spent the final 14 years of his life.

Peter Paul Rubens (1577–1640) was a seventeenth-century Flemish and European painter. He was known for his exuberant Baroque style that emphasized movement, color, and sensuality. He is well known for his portraits, landscapes, and paintings of mythological and symbolic subjects. His studio in Antwerp produced considerable numbers of paintings that were popular with the nobility and art collectors alike. *Rubenesque* is a term that has entered the language to describe corpulent and beautiful women of the kind that the artist frequently portrayed. Such was his fame that he was made a knight by both Philip IV, king of Spain, and Charles I, king of England.

A more contemporary Belgian artist is the surrealist René Magritte (1898–1967), whose strange and amusing images often

Peter Paul Rubens (*self-portrait, above*) gained fame for painting in a style that emphasized movement, color, and sensuality. In 2002, a newly discovered Rubens' painting called *Massacre of the Innocents* was sold at a Sotheby's auction for $76.2 million (£49.5 million), a record for an Old Master painting.

placed everyday objects out of context. Born at Lessines, he studied at the Académie Royale des Beaux-Arts in Brussels for two years, until 1918. His paintings presented paradoxes that might at first seem superficial but were frequently thought provoking. Good examples are his *The Son of Man* and *The Treachery of Images*. René Magritte described his paintings by saying: "My painting is visible images which conceal nothing; they evoke mystery and, indeed, when one sees one of my pictures, one asks oneself this simple question, 'What does that mean?' It does not mean anything, because mystery means nothing either; it is unknowable."

César Franck (1822–1890) was a composer, organist, and music teacher. Though born in Liège, he later lived in France. Although Franck's work was neglected during his lifetime, he has had a profound influence on music, including his role in resurrecting and giving renewed vigor to chamber music.

Henry van de Velde (1863–1957) was one of the main influences on Art Nouveau. His "New Art" was international in flavor and was extremely popular during the late nineteenth and early twentieth centuries. Van de Velde was gifted, being able to work with ease as a painter, an architect, and interior designer. He studied painting under masters both in Antwerp and Paris. By 1892, he had abandoned painting and turned his attention to interior design and decoration. Bloemenwerf, his own home located in Uccle near Brussels, was his first attempt at architecture. Much of his career was spent in Germany, where he had a strong influence on early twentieth century architecture and design. His Weimar School of Arts and Crafts in central Germany was the predecessor of the Bauhaus school. The Bauhaus greatly influenced modern architecture, the industrial and graphic arts, and theater design. During World War I, van de Velde left Germany and returned to Belgium. He continued his practice in architecture and design. By this time, however, he had abandoned the Art Nouveau phase of his career. The style had lost much of its popularity. During the chaotic years of World War I, van de Velde lived in Switzerland and the Netherlands. While in Holland, he designed the Kröller-Müller Museum. This well-known art museum, near the town of Otterlo, is home to the world's second-largest collection of paintings by Vincent van Gogh. Late in his career, van de Velde was a professor at Ghent University. While there, he was the architect of the Boekentoren, or Book Tower, the university's library.

When it comes to sports, there is one distinguished Belgian whose achievements top all others. Eddy Merckx, regarded as the greatest and most successful cyclist of all time, established several world cycling records, some of which remain unbroken to this day. He was elected Belgium's Sportsman of the Year an unprecedented six consecutive times in the years 1969 to 1974. He won the international Tour de France cycling race five times and would most likely have won a sixth had he not been attacked and punched by a Frenchman during the race. Many Frenchmen were upset that a Belgian might beat the record of five wins set by Frenchman Jacques Anquetil and regarded it as a matter of national honor to stop this from happening. Merckx was nicknamed "The Cannibal" because he seemed to devour his competition, and wanted to win every single race he participated in.

Merckx could be considered a perfect ambassador for Belgium, because he did not favor either Flanders or Wallonia but supported the unity of the country. This, together with his achievements in sports, pushed him to high rankings in both the Flemish (third) and Walloon (fourth) editions of the "Greatest Belgian" contest, held in 2005. In 1996, the Belgian king awarded him the title of Baron. In 2000, he was chosen Belgian "Sports Figure of the Century." Now retired, Merckx has become a good friend of U.S. Tour de France winner Lance Armstrong in recent years. After Armstrong won only his third Tour de France, Merckx predicted that the American would go on to win as many as seven Tours.

Two of the world's best female tennis champions, Justine Henin and Kim Clijsters, are Belgian.

Kim Clijsters became the first Belgian player, man or woman, to reach the number one spot, and is also one of the few women to be number one in both singles and doubles. She has won 41 singles titles and 4 Grand Slam singles titles. After a two-year retirement, Clijsters returned to the tour perhaps stronger than ever.

Due to her rare combination of power and grace, Justine Henin has been successful on the four main types of courts—clay, grass, indoor, and hard courts. She has won 43 career titles and 7 Grand Slam singles titles. She won the singles gold medal at the 2004 Summer Olympics. She retired from professional tennis in 2011.

5

Government and Politics

Belgium is a federal state in which amendments to the Constitution that were made in 1993 have resulted in a further reduction in the power of national government. What were formerly national powers have now been granted, at least to some degree, to regional and community governments. First, however, let us examine the various levels of government in Belgium.

FEDERAL GOVERNMENT

The Federal Parliament in Brussels consists of two chambers, the Belgian Senate and the Chamber of Representatives. The Senate (Dutch: de Senaat, French: le Sénat), or Upper House of Parliament, now comprises 71 elected senators. Forty are elected directly, 21 appointed by the community parliaments, and 10 are co-opted, or elected, by their fellow senators. Distribution of seats between the different political parties is the result of direct election. Before the federal Belgian election of May 1995, there were 184 elected senators. The 1993 reforms replaced the provincial senators, who were appointed by the provincial councils, with community senators.

The electorate is divided into two electoral colleges: one Dutch speaking and one French speaking. There is no German-speaking electoral college, as there is for European parliamentary elections. Instead, the members of Belgium's German-speaking community are considered part of the French electoral college. Despite the fact there are two electoral colleges, there are three actual constituencies in Senate elections: a Flemish constituency, a Wallonian constituency, and the constituency of Brussels-Halle-Vilvoorde, which includes the Brussels-Capital region and the surrounding part of the Flemish region.

Of the 40 directly elected senators, 25 are elected by the Dutch electoral college and 15 by the French electoral college. These numbers are fixed by the Belgian Constitution and roughly reflect the proportions of Dutch speakers and French speakers in the country. The directly elected senators are always elected on the same day as the members of the Chamber of Representatives, and for a term of four years unless the chambers are dissolved earlier. The most recent Belgian election took place in June 2007.

The lower house of Belgium's Federal Parliament is the Chamber of Representatives (Dutch: de Kamer van Volksvertegenwoordigers, French: la Chambre des Représentants). The chamber has 150 seats, a number determined by the Belgian Constitution. There are 11 electoral districts, each of which corresponds to one of the 10 Belgian provinces, except Flemish Brabant. That province is divided into two electoral districts: Brussels-Halle-Vilvoorde and Leuven. The number of seats for each electoral district is proportional to its population. All districts have an electoral threshold of 5 percent, except for the districts of Brussels-Halle-Vilvoorde and Leuven. This division results in five Dutch-speaking and five French-speaking electoral districts and the bilingual electoral district of Brussels-Halle-Vilvoorde.

With the rise of linguistic problems in the 1960s, each of the three
main political parties split into French- or Dutch-speaking parties.
Today all party candidates are exclusively Dutch or French speaking,
and representatives are not active in both communities. Pictured are
Crown Prince Philippe and Princess Mathilde casting their votes in the
2007 general elections.

The elected representatives are consequently divided into two language groups. Currently, of 150 total representatives, 88 are part of the Dutch-language group, which consists of the representatives from the Flemish areas. Another 62 are part of the French-language group, which consists of the representatives from the French-language and German-language areas. For the representatives from Brussels-Halle-Vilvoorde, the language in which they take their oath as a representative determines the language group to which they belong.

Because of the Belgian Constitution, both linguistic communities are granted equal powers in parliament. Although, in general, bills can be passed without a majority of both linguistic groups, bills that relate to specific issues (so-called "community laws") cannot. These require the consent of both language groups. The current president of the Chamber of Representatives is Herman Van Rompuy (Christian Democrat and Flemish).

The Chamber of Representatives elects a presiding officer, the president, at the beginning of each parliamentary term, which starts on the second Tuesday of October each year. The president is assisted by as many as five vice-presidents—two of whom are known respectively as the first vice-president and the second vice-president, who are also elected at the beginning of each parliamentary term. The president is customarily a member of one of the parties that forms the government coalition. The first vice-president is usually a member of the language group that the president does not represent.

The president presides over the plenary assembly of the Chamber of Representatives. He or she guides and controls debates in the assembly and is responsible for ensuring the democratic functioning of the chamber, for the maintenance of order and security in the assembly, and for enforcing the rules of the Chamber of Representatives. To this end, he or she is given considerable powers. He or she also represents the chamber at both the national and the international level. Finally, the president assesses the admissibility of bills and proposals.

ROLE OF THE KING

The president of the Chamber of Representatives and the president of the Belgian Senate rank immediately behind the king in the order of precedence; the elder of the two presidents takes second place. The presidents of the Chamber of Representatives and the Senate rank above the prime minister.

At this point, we should note that the Senate lost most of its power to the Chamber of Representatives as a result of the 1993 constitutional amendments. The king also lost his power to dissolve parliament, making Belgium's constitutional monarchy even more of a ceremonial office than it was previously. The Belgian monarchy combines both public and political missions. From a public point of view, the king symbolizes and maintains national unity by representing the country in public functions and at international meetings.

The king does, however, have a number of responsibilities with regard to the government's formation. The process usually begins with the king's nomination of an *informateur*. This individual informs the king of the main political formations that may be available for governance. Following this phase, the king can appoint another informateur or a *formateur*, who will have the charge of forming a new government, for which he or she generally becomes prime minister.

The king has the right to meet with the prime minister regularly so that he can exercise the power of warning and advice (due to the length of the king's reign, this can become very important—as with Baudouin I, who was considered the best informed Belgian). The king is also the commander of the Belgian army, although his role is largely ceremonial. Until Leopold III, the king commanded the army in person, in the field.

Finally, Belgians can write to their king when they encounter difficulties with the administrative powers. This is a well-known option for those who come up against governmental stubbornness, but there is little record of this option having resolved many such difficulties.

SUBNATIONAL GOVERNMENT

We have considered the national government of Belgium and how it is organized. Next, we should also look at the subnational level and the complexities of government in a federal state that is divided by language in a way that is unlike nearly any other country. Belgium has four levels of subnational government. First is community government, which is divided into Dutch speaking, French speaking and German speaking. Second is regional government, for Flanders, Wallonia, and the Brussels-Capital region. Third is the provincial government of the 10 provinces. The fourth, and lowest, level is communal government, which comprises 589 municipalities or communes. These municipalities are the smallest administrative subdivisions of Belgium.

The communities, regions, language areas, provinces, and municipalities are the five most important subnational entities of Belgium, as laid out into the Belgian Constitution. Lesser subnational entities include, for instance, the intra-municipal districts; the administrative, the electoral, and the judicial *arrondissements* (small administrative subdistricts); and police districts, as well as the new inter-municipal police zones (which rank below police districts).

All of the five main entities have geographical boundaries. The language areas have no offices or powers as such and exist only as precise geographical definitions, serving to delimit whatever subdivisions are empowered. The institutional communities are thus equally geographically determined: The Flemish government has legal authority only within the areas of the Flemish and Brussels region; the French-speaking community has powers only within the areas of the Walloon and Brussels region. Belgian communities do not refer directly to groups of people—there is, indeed, no subnationality in Brussels—but rather to specific political, linguistic, and cultural competencies, or responsibilities of the country.

As a result, all communities have a precise and legally established area in which they can exercise their competencies.

The Flemish community is competent in the Dutch-speaking regions and the bilingual area of Brussels-Capital; the French-speaking community in the French-language area of the Walloon region and the Brussels-Capital region; and the German community in the German-language area, a small part of the province of Liège in the Walloon region bordering Germany with its capital at Eupen.

POLITICAL PARTIES

Ever since the creation of the Belgian state in 1830 and throughout most of the nineteenth century, its politics have been dominated by just two political parties: the Catholic Party and the Liberal Party. The former has always been seen as politically conservative and closely oriented with the Roman Catholic Church. The latter has generally taken an anticlerical standpoint and is politically progressive. In the late 1800s, the Socialist Party arose to represent the Belgian working class who labored in the many new industries. Today, these three groups still dominate Belgian politics, but each of them has evolved in character in different ways. There are also nationalist parties, principally Flemish, and a Green Party.

Because Belgium is a federation with a multiparty political system, there are numerous small parties that have little chance of gaining power alone. They must work together in some way to form coalition governments if they wish to avoid always being in opposition.

The complexity of Belgian politics is compounded by the fact that all Belgian political parties are divided into linguistic groups: Flemish, French, or German. The Flemish parties operate in Flanders and the Brussels-Capital region, the French-speaking ones in Wallonia and the Brussels-Capital region, and some German-speaking parties operate in the small German-speaking community.

Thus, political parties are invariably organized along community lines; no representative parties operate in both the Flemish and Walloon communities. Even in Brussels, all the parties that put forward candidates are either Flemish or French speaking, and this situation reflects the duality of Belgian society. Consequently, there are no parties in existence now that operate on a completely national level. After World War II, the national Catholic Party severed its ties to the Church and became a mass party of the center, similar to a political party in the United States. It was renamed the Christian Democratic Party, but this unity was not to last for much longer than two decades.

Until 1968, the Christian Democratic Party was indeed a national political force; however, in response to Belgium's linguistic tensions, it divided into two independent parties. These were the Christelijke Volkspartij (CVP) in Flanders and the Parti Social Chrétien (PSC) in French-speaking Belgium. Both parties have the same basic policies but are completely separate organizations. The CVP is larger than the PSC and usually attracts about twice the number of votes. These parties always formed an alliance in coalition government but were ousted from office in 1999 after 40 years in government. More recently, the CVP has changed its name to Christen-Democratisch en Vlaams (CD&V), and the PSC has become Centre Démocrate Humaniste (cdH). Small, breakaway liberal-conservative parties were formed after 1999, in both Flanders and Wallonia, but these soon joined the major liberal parties in their respective regions.

Jean-Luc Dehaene, who was Belgian prime minister from 1992 to 1995, led a coalition of his own Christian Democrats and Social Democrats. This became one of Belgium's most important governments, because it successfully transformed Belgium into a federal state in 1993. Then, from 1995 to 1999, he led a second coalition government with a similar composition. This administration was plagued by crises, including the infamous Affaire Dutroux scandal, to which we shall return later.

In recent years, most Belgian Socialist parties have shed the Marxist (Socialist) ideologies in which they were deeply rooted. Although they are still closely linked to organized labor and

Talbia Belhouari, a 2007 Socialist Party candidate for the Chamber of Deputies, has been active in the fight for immigrant women's rights and to combat discrimination. She was the first candidate to launch an ecological campaign using recyclable posters that can be reused for three successive election campaigns.

trade unions, the Socialists have adopted more centrist positions with regard to policies. This makes the Belgian Socialist parties largely similar to the German Social Democrats and the French Socialist Party. Nevertheless, they too split along linguistic lines in 1978. The French-speaking Parti Socialiste (PS) is principally based in the industrial cities of Charleroi, Mons, and Liège in Wallonia. The Flemish Socialist Party, whose support is less regionally concentrated, became the Socialistische Partij anders (SP.a) in 2002.

The Socialists have participated in several postwar governments and produced some of Belgium's most distinguished statesmen. The Socialists in Wallonia have focused primarily on domestic issues, whereas the Flemish Socialists have tended to concentrate on international issues. In the past, the latter have been strident critics with regard to issues of European security, and they often opposed U.S. policies. In recent years, however, under the guidance of three Flemish Socialist foreign ministers—Willy Claes, Frank Vandenbroucke, and Erik Derycke—the party has moved firmly toward the center and has taken less controversial positions on foreign policy issues. As with other European Socialist parties, there have been defections by left-wing elements. This has been true particularly with regard to those who object to the "watering down" of Socialism and similar groups within the SP.a and PS who are trying to regain control.

Besides the Christian Democrats and the Socialists, liberal parties also exist in Belgium. These appeal mainly to business-people, the self-employed, shopkeepers, property owners, and those who are conservatively inclined. Belgian liberalism is of a moderate, centrist, and conservative variety. Like the other political parties, the liberals are divided along linguistic lines. The Flemish Liberals and Democrats, the Vlaamse Liberalen en Democraten (VLD), are currently the largest political force in Belgium. The VLD is at present headed by Bart Somers. During the 1990s, the party chairman was Guy Verhofstadt, who became prime minister in 1999. The French-speaking Reformist Movement, the Mouvement Réformateur (MR), is headed by Didier Reynders. The MR is a federation of a split-off wing of the Christian Democrats Mouvement des Citoyens pour le Changement (MCC) and the Brussels-based Front Démocratique des Francophones (FDF), which has a strong electoral share in the capital region.

Until the general election of June 2007, a coalition of Liberals and Socialists governed the country with a sufficient majority in parliament. The election resulted in a considerable upset for the status quo. Guy Verhofstadt, who had held office as prime minister since 1999, was forced to resign when his governing VLD Liberals and their Socialist partners suffered big losses. For the previous eight years, the VLD and its partners had formed a "purple coalition" government under him.

Following Guy Verhofstadt's resignation, a 100-day power-vacuum occurred, during which the country was without leadership. Finally, Verhofstadt was reappointed prime minister as head of an interim government. He was replaced in 2008 by Yves Leterme, leader of the Christian Democratic and Flemish party (CD&V). Within months, Leterme was swept up in a financial crisis and scandal and resigned. He was replaced by Christian Democrat Herman Van Rompuy, who left office within months to become President of the European Council. Yves Leterme replaced him as Prime Minister, but resigned in early 2010 resulting in the government once again collapsing.

No party, however, ever wins a Belgian election outright. Consensus is important, and the Flemish Christian Democrats, along with their French speaking sister party, must forge a sustainable coalition with at least one other group. In 2010, the separatist New Flemish Alliance became the largest political party and the French Socialist Party gained power in Wallonia. There is never a dull moment in Belgian politics.

THE EUROPEAN UNION

Whatever national government holds power in Brussels, the greater power of the European Union (EU) also administers its very considerable empire from the same city. From its smaller beginnings as the European Economic Community (EEC) in 1957, this organization has grown enormously in a half century—from an initial membership of 6 states to 27 since 2007. This new phase of EU expansion followed the signing of the Treaty of Maastricht (in the Netherlands) in 1992. This treaty led to the creation of the European Union, and to the dropping of the former name. It was principally the result of separate negotiations toward monetary and political union. From this point forward, some EU leaders firmly set their sights on political union and the eventual creation of a federal European state.

The combined economy of the EU now is the largest in the world, with a nominal GDP of $19.9 trillion in 2010. The EU has a single market among member states with a common trade policy, a Common Agricultural and Fisheries Policy, and a firmly established regional development policy. Its common standard currency, the euro, has now been adopted by 13 of the member states—including Belgium, which switched over in 2002. Since 1993, the EU has begun to develop a limited Common Foreign and Security Policy, as well as cooperation in police and judicial matters. The Common Security Policy may lead to the creation of a multinational EU military force that could be used in appropriate circumstances.

THE BELGIAN MONARCHY

To conclude this chapter on Belgian government and the complexities that are forced on it by the linguistic divisions that exist within the country, we should consider how this affects the head of state, the king of the Belgians. This, incidentally, is the correct title, and not "king of Belgium"; the intention is to link the monarchy to the Belgian people rather than to the country. This implies a popular monarchy, whereas the former title might be seen to indicate a constitutional or absolute monarchy that is linked to territory and state.

As a result of the First World War, King Albert I decided in 1920 to no longer use the name Saxe-Coburg-Gotha as the official family name of the Belgian royal family. The decision was made without publicity and was not enacted in an official royal decree. Therefore, there is some confusion in other countries, and even in Belgium, that Saxe-Coburg-Gotha is the family name still used by the Belgian royals. The family name was changed to van België (Dutch), de Belgique (French), and von Belgien (German). Because Belgium is a country with three official languages, the name was chosen to employ all three versions, with none having precedence over the others. This probably makes the Belgian royals the only family in the world with three different, but equally valid, family names.

The Royal Palace of Brussels is one of the capital's most striking official buildings. It faces the Belgian Parliament, at the other end of the Parc Royal. The Royal Palace symbolizes Belgium's constitutional monarchy, but it is not where the king actually lives. Instead, the palace is where the king has his office and exercises his prerogative as head of state. It is also where the king grants audiences and deals with affairs of state. The Royal Palace is home to the services of the grand marshal of the court and the head of the king's guards. Inside the palace are the magnificent state rooms, where prestigious receptions are held, as well as the apartments that are made available to heads of state during their official visits.

Since 1965, it has been a tradition for the Royal Palace of Brussels to open its doors to the public once every year. Visits are permitted during the summer months, just after July 21, the Belgian National Holiday. However, it is in the suburb of Laken (French: Laeken), just outside the city center, that one finds the Chateau de Laeken, the actual residence of the king and queen. Albert von Sachsen-Teschen, the governor of the Austrian Netherlands, built this palace as his residence in 1772. After the French took power in the southern Netherlands, it was purchased by Napoleon in 1804. Following the battle of Waterloo in 1815, it next became the property of King William I, king of the United Netherlands. Fifteen years later, when Belgium became an independent state, the palace was presented to King Leopold I as a gift from the Belgian nation. Following a fire in 1890, it was rebuilt and enlarged, and it became the permanent residence of the royal family during the reign of King Leopold III.

6

Belgium's Economy

Belgium is located in one of the most industrialized areas of Europe. Because of its industrial strength—and hence, employment opportunities—it is also one of the most densely populated. The per capita gross national product (GNP) for the Flemish and Central regions ranks among the highest in the entire European Union (EU); the average figure for the Walloon region is approximately 25 percent less. As Belgium enters the twenty-first century, the economy has a dynamic service sector with strength comparable to that of the other leading European powers. Today, about 75 percent of the nation's economy is based on the provision of services, and three of every four jobs are in the service sector. Agriculture, once important, now accounts for little more than 1 percent of the labor force. Clearly, Belgium has made the transition from an economy based on agriculture and industry to one dependent on postindustrial activities.

EARLY INDUSTRIAL GROWTH

Together with Britain, Belgium was a leader of the Industrial Revolution during the early nineteenth century. The first heavy industries, such as coal mining and steelmaking, grew during the decades that followed Belgian independence in 1830. These prospered until well after World War II, before the oil crises of the 1970s depressed the economy and started a recession. The mining industry was principally centered in the Walloon cities of Charleroi and Liège, where there were large coal deposits. Consequently, steelmaking plants were built in the same areas to make use of this fuel. There are also coalfields north of Ghent, in East Flanders. The decline of these industries is the principal reason for the slowing of economic development in Wallonia and a shift of economic wealth to the north part of the country. The area that includes Brussels, Ghent, and Antwerp has become the main focus of recent economic development. This is the reason for the shift in per capita GNP that now favors the Flemish north.

MANUFACTURING

Belgium's manufacturing industry now accounts for about half the value of the country's exports. Most of the raw materials used in the country's industries, however, must be imported. This is the case with steelmaking and the production of other metals, which mainly use ores from abroad. In Europe, Belgium is one of the principal industrial refiners and producers of metals like cobalt and radium and the metalloid germanium. It is also a leader in the chemical and petrochemical industries. Plastics made from petroleum products are manufactured on a large scale, and glassmaking is another Belgian industry.

About 80 percent of all diamonds marketed in the world come from Antwerp, where the raw stones are imported for processing. Professional diamond buyers, diamond dealers, diamond brokers, and jewelry manufacturers have made the city the center of the world's diamond industry. In the

Antwerp, Belgium, has been the home of the diamond industry for the past five centuries. Millions of diamonds worth billions of dollars pass through the hands of highly skilled diamond workers, including the best polishers in the world. This employee is cutting diamonds before they get polished.

sixteenth century, Antwerp was a flourishing and expanding city that already played a major role in the development of diamond cutting and polishing techniques. During the 1500s, for example, King Francois I of France did not call on the diamond cutters of Paris; rather, he placed his orders with the craftsmen of Antwerp.

The manufacture of heavy machinery and automobiles plays a significant role in the Belgian economy. Four well-known international carmakers have major production and assembly units here: Ford in Genk, Opel in Antwerp, Volvo Cars in Ghent, and Volkswagen in Brussels. Their combined average annual output of vehicles exceeds 880,000 units, with a total value of approximately $13 billion. As a result, Belgium is still a world leader in terms of per capita annual production of motor vehicles. More than 96 percent of this output is for export, further emphasizing the international character of the industry. The parent companies have all confirmed their confidence in Belgium by means of ongoing and sustained capital expenditure programs.

ENERGY

Obviously, the Belgian economy, together with many other aspects of modern life, depends on sufficient energy supplies. About 70 percent of Belgium's electricity is generated by nuclear power plants. The rest comes from hydroelectric power, which is generated in the Ardennes. In 2003, the government voted to close down the country's seven nuclear power plants by 2025. Because of its relatively flat terrain, Belgium has limited hydroelectric potential. Therefore, the country will have to increase its use of alternative energy sources. These include atmosphere-fouling and increasingly costly petroleum, natural gas, and coal, or unsightly wind turbines.

The national electricity grid is interconnected with those of neighboring EU countries. This allows power, when needed, to be supplied by sources outside the country. Belgium's surplus electrical energy also can be exported to these other countries.

Petroleum from the North Sea oil fields and the Middle East is refined in Antwerp. This is the second largest port in Europe and the fifth largest in the world. It handles most of Belgium's overseas trade and is the destination for many giant tanker vessels that bring oil from around the world. Antwerp and Ghent are both centers for the petroleum and chemical industries following massive expansion in these sectors after World War II. In recent years, both oil and natural gas imports to Belgium have increased. Most of the supplies come from Russia and other parts of the former Soviet Union.

TRANSPORTATION

Located in the heart of the EU, Belgium's economy is well suited to integration of its industry with that of neighboring countries. It is able to achieve this openness through extensive highway and rail networks, most of which radiate outward from Brussels. Modern expressways link all of the main cities in the country and the major cities of the neighboring Netherlands, France, and Germany.

The state-owned Belgian National Railways offers fast and frequent service to all of the main centers of population. The Thalys high-speed train takes only 85 minutes to travel between Paris and Brussels. This covers the distance of 210 miles (336 kilometers) at an average speed of 148 mph (237 kilometers/hour). Twenty-five Thalys trains depart daily in each direction between Paris and Brussels. The Eurostar train service from Brussels to London, England, via the Channel Tunnel currently takes 2 hours and 45 minutes. A new Eurostar service between the two cities that began in late 2007 reduced the journey's travel time to 1 hour and 51 minutes. Such rapid rail transport between EU capital cities is most competitive with corresponding air travel and is seen as a considerable asset to modern business.

Nevertheless, air travel to and from Belgium plays a major transportation role between this country and other EU countries, and also more distant destinations. Large international airports at Brussels and Antwerp serve many foreign airlines. Sabena, Belgium's national airline, went bankrupt in November 2001. This resulted from the severe airline recession caused by the September 11 attacks on the United States.

Quite apart from road and rail travel, the canals of Belgium have for centuries carried many industrial cargoes, and they still do. These canals are mostly located in the northern part of the country, and today they are fully modernized to handle European-size barges. The original purpose of the canals was to enable the transport of heavy industrial loads by water. Today, however, they have also become popular cruising and boating vacations. Waterborne tourists are well catered to on the canals

Although farming amounts to little more than one percent of total labor, livestock and dairy farming are major agricultural industries. Belgium's moderate temperatures, evenly distributed precipitation, and long growing season make conditions ideal for harvesting sugar beets, potatoes, fruits, flax, and grains.

that connect Nieuwpoort, Bruges, Ghent, Ypres, and many other Belgian towns.

OTHER INDUSTRIES

Farming in Belgium is mainly concerned with rearing livestock. Consequently, much of the country's arable land is used as pasture or for growing fodder. The amount of grain planted for human consumption is fairly minimal in the country. Just over

1 percent of Belgium's labor force is engaged in agriculture, which is why it only accounts for a small fraction of the country's income. About 21 percent of the area of Belgium is forested, and there is a substantial lumber industry. The annual value of lumber exports exceeds US$3 billion.

Brewing is a major industry, and Belgian beer has earned considerable prestige. There are about 125 breweries in the country with an annual production of about one-half billion U.S. gallons (18,927,060 hectoliters). Some 60 percent of all Belgian beer is exported. Belgians consume an average 25 gallons (93 liters) of beer annually, which contributes to a lively economy based upon the popular beverage.

Belgium's fishing industry is comparatively small, but there are a number of trawlers that operate in the North Sea. These are principally based in Ostend, which is the country's chief fishing port. The catch is mainly herring and flatfish, which include flounder, sole, plaice, and halibut. The industry is able to supply about 30 percent of the country's market for fish.

The textile industry used to be a major force in the 1970s, when it employed more than 90,000 people. During recent years, however, it has gone into sharp decline, currently employing fewer than a quarter of that number. Ghent is the main center for the production of cotton and artificial fibers, and linen production is centered in Kortrijk. Verviers is known for its woolen industry. As noted earlier, Bruges was for 200 years a great center of the lace-making industry, which brought the city considerable prosperity. Until fairly recently, this was a dying craft, but the industry has been reenergized; once again, Bruges is the lace-making capital of Europe.

MEDIA

The Belgian press is made up of more than 35 daily newspapers, which are controlled by various groups. The circulation of these newspapers obviously depends on readership, which will either be Dutch speaking or French speaking. Because many people are multilingual, the major journals are available in all parts of the country. There is also a German-language daily newspaper.

In a similar manner, there are Dutch-speaking terrestrial TV and radio channels that are broadcast nationally, as well as French-speaking channels. Many other commercial TV channels are available via cable access, and there are also satellite channels. The European Union's TV information service, Europe by Satellite (EbS), was launched in 1995. Its TV and radio stations provide EU-related pictures and sound in more than 21 languages. The programming consists of a mix of live events, stock shots, and finished programs on EU subjects produced by various EU institutions and directorates, as well as from other broadcasters. Much of what is broadcast by EbS originates in Brussels.

BELGIUM'S INTERNATIONAL ECONOMIC LINKS

As we have seen, Belgium's economy is highly diversified and strongly oriented toward foreign trade. Most of its exports are based on high-value, low-bulk goods to which value is added by skilled and often highly specialized labor, such as cut diamonds. The main imports are food products, petroleum and petroleum products, chemicals, machinery, textiles, clothing, and uncut diamonds. Principal exports are automobiles, iron and steel, nonferrous metals, petroleum products, plastics, textiles, and finished diamonds.

Since 1922, Belgium and its neighbor Luxembourg have been a single trade market within a common customs and currency union, known as the Belgium-Luxembourg Economic Union. Following the advent of the European Union, a similar trend has resulted in customs and frontier posts between Belgium and its EU neighbors largely being removed. Today, one can usually cross these national borders via highways without passport controls or stopping for customs inspection. Travel is as free and open as it is between U.S. states or Canadian provinces.

In 2002, Belgium replaced its unit of national currency, the Belgian franc, with the euro, the single European currency. Euros had been introduced as valid currency three years earlier. This step removed any requirement for currency exchange and differential rates of exchange with the EU states that had also adopted the euro. Clearly this was a major advantage with regard to foreign trade between Belgium and fellow EU member states. Some EU members, like the United Kingdom, opted not to adopt the euro as a single currency. They were afraid that adoption of the currency would be a major step toward more complete economic and political integration. In contrast, Belgium, a founding member of the EU, strongly supports the extension of the powers of EU institutions to integrate the member economies.

Symbolic of Belgium's economic power following the inauguration of the European Economic Community (which was to develop into the mighty EU) was the Brussels World Fair of 1958. Sometimes known as Expo '58, this showcase for science, trade, and industry was the first major world fair to be held following World War II.

Nearly 15,000 workers spent three years building the nearly one square mile (2 square kilometers) site on the Heysel Plateau, 4½ miles (7 kilometers) northwest of the capital. The site is best known for its giant model of a unit cell of an iron crystal (each sphere representing an iron atom), called the Atomium. This consists of nine giant metal-clad spheres, each 59 feet (18 meters) in diameter and joined by tubes that contain escalators. The whole futuristic structure weighs 2,400 tons and stands 335 feet (102 meters) high. Originally planned to last only six months, architect André Waterkeyn's design has survived to become a popular tourist attraction that some feel is a national icon—Belgium's equivalent of Paris's Eiffel Tower. It sits close to the King Baudouin Stadium in Heysel Park, next to the Congress Centre and the Mini-Europe

Park. Nearly 50 years later, the Atomium remains one of the best-known landmarks in Brussels. More than 45 million people have visited the World Fair site, which opened with a call for world peace and social and economic progress issued by King Baudouin I.

7

Living in Belgium Today

I t is sometimes said that many people in Europe hold a rather negative image of Belgium. Undoubtedly, the country is sharply divided by language. This division causes a seemingly endless separation of people, politics, government, administration, media, and other aspects of society and culture. It is a densely populated country and one that is often described as being flat, dull, and boring. As in other northern European countries, it often seems that it is always raining here.

QUALITY OF LIFE

Yet, despite these negative impressions, Belgians have a consistently high quality of life. In 2009, Belgium ranked seventeenth among the world's 182 countries listed in the prestigious Human Develop Index (HDI). This widely acclaimed index uses a number of categories to measure human well-being. (Canada ranks fourth on the HDI and the U.S. is thirteenth on the list). In 2010, Brussels ranked fifteenth among world cities rated by Mercer Human Resource Consulting. By comparison, Ottawa and Toronto, Canada, ranked fourteenth and sixteenth respectively. The only U.S. cities even close to Brussels' ranking were Honolulu, Hawaii, (thirty-first) and San Francisco, California (thirty-second).

The gross domestic product (GDP) growth for 2006 was 3.2 percent. This figure represented a record leap in the history of the country's economy. By 2008, the Belgian economy began to falter in response to the global economic downturn. In 2009, the country's GDP suffered a 3.1 percent decline. Per capita incomes and gross domestic product experienced little change during the last years of the decade. As the decade drew to a close, Belgium's per capita GDP-PPP was $36,600, ranking twenty-ninth among the world's nations. This relative prosperity extends throughout the country, although figures for productivity show that it is, on average, 10 percent greater for the inhabitants of the Flemish regions in the north compared with the Wallonians in the south.

Brussels, which is the multilingual and multiethnic capital, is more than just the huge central metropolis of this country. It calls itself, with reason, the "Capital of Europe," and the very name "Brussels" is now synonymous with the parliament of the European Union (EU). On TV and in the news media around the world, we continually hear that "Brussels reaches a decision" or "Brussels issues a ruling." Yet, how much does all the debating and decision-making have to do with the country and its people?

As we have said, the quality of life in Belgium is rated higher than in many U.S. cities; certainly, this is a prosperous country by any standards. To assess what this means for Belgian citizens, we should briefly examine key aspects of modern life such as housing, education, culture, cuisine,

The European Union (EU) as we now know it was formally established on November 1, 1993. Belgium is one of the six founding members of the EU's predecessor, the European Economic Community (EEC). Today, more than 500 million citizens and 27 member countries make up the EU. Pictured is the headquarters for the European Commission, the executive branch of the EU.

entertainment, and sports. We should also consider negative aspects, such as crime.

Housing

Reasonably priced housing is still widely available in Belgium, despite steep rises in real estate prices during recent years. These increases, following five years of solid growth, have been most noticeable in Brussels. In 2004, the average house price in Brussels was $228,000. This made it the cheapest European capital, trailing London ($410,000) and Paris ($326,000). The quoted figures are calculated using the exchange rate of 1 euro = 1.25 U.S. dollars, which was roughly the rate at the time. However, realtors say house prices began to rise sharply in the Belgian capita and elsewhere throughout the country in 2005 and continued to rise throughout the remainder of the decade. These price rises were attributed mainly to low interest rates. A wide choice of rental accommodations is also available, ranging from studio apartments to villas in Brussels and its suburbs. Whereas prices do not match those of many other European cities, housing costs are now less a bargain than in the past.

Medical Services

Another benefit of living in Belgium is its excellent medical services, which are among the most modern in the world. The country has about 40,000 doctors to serve the needs of its 10.5 million citizens, and approximately 400 hospitals are scattered throughout the country along with a large number of specialist centers.

Belgium's medical services are known for their easy accessibility, low cost, and high standards. In fact, every year about 20,000 people from other European countries who are experiencing long delays in receiving treatment travel to Belgium to get medical care. This is one advantage of being a member of the European Union. European Community law states that any citizen of the Union who is enduring "undue delays" in receiving treatment in their home country can apply to have medical care in a member-state. Even with travel expenses added in, this can be a real bargain.

Education

Education in Belgium is regulated and for the most part financed by one of the three communities—Flemish, Walloon, or German. All three communities have a unified school system that features only small differences with regard to organization. The particular types of schools are further divided into three groups. First, there are schools owned by the communities. Second, there are subsidized public schools organized by provinces and municipalities. Finally, there are subsidized free schools, most of which are administered by an organization that is affiliated with the Catholic Church. The latter group,

In the past, Dutch was considered the language of peasants by Belgium's French-speaking majority. Today an increasing number of French-speaking parents are sending their children to Dutch-language schools because of their smaller classes and better resources. Unemployment is high in French-speaking Brussels, whereas in the province of Brabant, Dutch-speaking workers are desperately needed.

parochial schools, is the largest in both the number of schools and the number of pupils.

Education in Belgium is compulsory between the ages of 6 and 18. School results in Belgium compare favorably with other European countries. Dutch-speaking students generally perform somewhat better on standardized tests than do French-speaking ones. The different stages of education are the same in all communities. Basic education consists of preschool (up to 6 years) followed by primary school (6 to 12 years). Although it is not compulsory, more than 90 percent of all children attend preschool, which—like primary school—is free. Education in primary schools is rather traditional: It concentrates on reading, writing, and basic mathematics, but it also touches upon a very broad range of topics that includes biology, music, religion, history, and geography.

Flemish schools in Brussels and some municipalities near the language border must offer French lessons beginning in the first or second year. Most other Flemish schools offer French education during the third cycle. Primary schools in the French community must teach a foreign language, which is generally Dutch or English, depending on the school. Primary schools in the German community include obligatory French lessons.

Secondary school is for 12- to 18-year-old students. When they graduate from primary school around the age of 12, students enter secondary education. At this point, they have to choose a direction that they want to follow, depending on their skill level and interests. This direction will be either general secondary education, or technical or vocational (both of which are very job specific).

Higher education in Belgium is organized by the two main communities: the Flemish and the French. German speakers typically enroll in institutions in the French community, or in Germany. In Belgium, anyone who has a qualifying diploma of secondary education is free to enroll at any institute of higher education, typically universities or colleges. There, students work toward earning a bachelor's degree, which usually takes three years. This may be followed by another one to two years of work to earn a master's degree. This is in line with the Bologna Process, which has become the standard for many European countries. Financial aid is available for students whose families lack sufficient income. The aid is awarded by the community governments and depends on the family's financial circumstances, but it is seldom more than $4,000 per year.

Information Technology

One aspect of modern life in which Belgium, like most other EU nations, is at the forefront is the use of computers and the Internet. The total population of the EU in 2010 was approximately 489 million (of the world's 6.830 billion people), or 7.2 percent of the world's population. The number of EU citizens who are Internet users was approximately 320 million in 2010, or about 18 percent of the world's total Internet users (over 1.8 billion in 2010). Internet usage in the EU population as a whole is 65 percent, compared to only 24 percent for the rest of the world. In Belgium, about 70 percent of the population uses the Internet. These figures indicate a population that is generally well educated and eager to embrace new information technology. It may also signal a new willingness to bridge the gap caused by Belgium's linguistic diversity.

CULTURAL LIFE

Belgium is rich in culture. Most Belgians view their culture as an integral part of European, or Western, culture. Even so, both the Walloons and the Flemish tend to make individual and collective cultural choices mainly from within their own community. When they do go outside their community, the Flemish draw intensively from the English-speaking culture (which dominates sciences, professional life, and most news media) and French and other Latin cultures. The French speakers, however, tend to focus on cultural life in Paris and elsewhere in the French-speaking world.

Cinema and Theater

A wide variety of cinema options exist, especially in Brussels. Movies made in the United States are generally screened in their original English, and many French-made films are shown in Belgium. Belgian filmmakers have been rewarded quite a few times at the Cannes Film Festival (for example, the filmmaking duo Luc and Jean-Pierre Dardenne, Benoît Poelvoorde, and others) and also in other less-known festivals. Belgian movies are generally made on a fairly low budget.

Belgian theater is likewise divided between the two communities, and each has developed in its own way. Even at arts festivals, such as that mounted by the Belgian government in 1980 to mark the five-hundredth anniversary of the founding of Brussels, this divide was starkly evident. It was particularly noticeable to foreign correspondents who were primarily invited to the French-language plays, which they were more likely to understand. Most plays are performed in French, but there is also a lively Dutch language theater scene to be found.

Museums and Galleries

Belgium has many impressive museums and art galleries, which draw members of the Belgian public and tourists alike. Particularly of note are the four museums connected with the Royal Museums of Fine Arts of Belgium. These are situated in the capital, in the downtown area of the Coudenberg. Two of the museums (the Museum of Ancient Art and the Museum of Modern Art) are located in the main building. The other two (the Museum Constantin Meunier and the Antoine Wiertz Museum) are dedicated to specific Belgian artists. These are much smaller and are located in different areas of the city. The main building is the largest museum complex in Belgium.

Located in the heart of Brussels, this museum contains a rich collection of fourteenth-century fine arts and artifacts. Its prized possessions are numerous works confiscated by the French revolutionaries in 1794, the collections of King William I, and independent works of art by Belgian artists since 1830.

The Royal Museum of Fine Arts (Dutch: Koninklijk Museum von Schone Kunsten) in Antwerp is another museum with a magnificent collection, including works by Jan van Eyck, Peter Paul Rubens, Anthony van Dyck, Franz Hals, and Auguste Rodin among others. A haven for art lovers is the Groeninge Museum in Bruges. This museum offers a rich and fascinating array of works, primarily by Belgian artists. Highlights include the world-famous collection of works by the Flemish Primitives, as well as paintings by various Renaissance and Baroque masters. There are several interesting pieces from the Neoclassical and Realist periods of the eighteenth and nineteenth centuries. Among the collections can be found milestones from the Symbolist and Modernist movements, masterpieces by the Flemish Expressionists, and a varied selection of post-1945 modern art. Works included are by artists such as Hiëronymus Bosch, Jean Brusselmans, Petrus Christus, Emile Claus, Gerard David, Gustave de Smet, James Ensor, René Magritte, Hans Memling, Constant Permeke, Jan van Eyck, Rik Wouters, and many others.

Belgian Cuisine

We have already discussed some of the food for which this country justly prides itself. It is sometimes said that Belgians prefer quantity rather than quality with regard to food, which is why one is likely to be given large helpings. Even so, when it comes to eating out in restaurants, Belgium can provide unrivalled choice and quality as well. Brussels is said to have more Michelin Guide starred restaurants than even Paris.

Brussels sprouts may be a plain vegetable, but more popular foods have been introduced by the Belgians, namely waffles and French fries despite the name of the latter. One of the typical Belgian dishes is *stoemp* (mashed potatoes with other vegetables, often served with sausage). The country is also well known for *vlaamse stoofkarbonaden* (French: *carbonnades fla-mandes*), or Flemish beef stew. This dish is made like French beef burgundy, but using beer instead of red wine. Of course, there are the ubiquitous mussels and fries, called *moules frites* in French or *mosselen friet* in Dutch. Belgian pâté as well as other cold meat products from the Ardennes are also a source of pride in restaurants throughout the country.

Belgian beer is renowned for its quality. Its importance to the Belgians is comparable to that of wine to the French or Italians. For a small nation, Belgium has perhaps the most numerous and varied selection of beers in the world. Best known abroad are the popular pale lagers, but one can also find specialized brews like Flemish Red and lambic beers, which have distinctive tart flavors. Belgian beer brewing goes back to medieval times, when monasteries began producing beers. Trappist beers, of which there are six varieties in Belgium brewed by Trappist monks, are very popular. The monks have taken a vow of silence and will not reveal their recipe, yet their brewing expertise appears to be undiminished.

One of the oldest breweries in the country is the Den Horen Brewery in the city of Leuven, which can be traced back to 1366. In 1708, Sebastian Artois became master brewer and later gave his name to the brewery. Today, the Artois Brewery, which existed long before Belgium became an independent nation, is best known for its Stella Artois lager. The beer is exported worldwide, and, in 2006, the brewery's production reached 10 million hectoliters (about 264,000,000 U.S. gallons).

Beer production was boosted by a 1919 parliamentary act that prohibited the sale of spirits in pubs, thus encouraging the market to produce beers that contained a higher level of alcohol. There are indeed thousands of pubs in Belgium—where they are called cafés—and most of these offer a wide selection of beer, which is mostly bottled rather than draft.

Celebrations

Festivals play a major role in Belgium's cultural life. Nearly every city and town has its own festival, and many date back several centuries. These aren't just displays put on to encourage tourism but real, authentic celebrations that take months to prepare. Two of the biggest festivals are the three-day carnival at Binche, near Mons, which is held just before Lent (the 40 days that precede Easter), and the Procession of the Holy Blood, held in Bruges in May. During the carnival in Binche, *gilles* lead the procession. These are men dressed in high, plumed hats and bright costumes. Several of these festivals include sporting competitions, such as cycling, and many of the celebrations are known as *kermesse* festivals. *Kermesse* is an old Flemish word derived from *kerk* (church) and *mis* (mass). These festivals were originally organized by local churches and were accompanied by feasting, dancing, and sports. Now they are now more like town fairs, and nearly every village has such a festival once or twice a year. The large Zuidfoor, or Foire du Midi (South Fair), of Brussels and the Sinksenfoor (Whitsun Fair) of Antwerp attract many visitors over several weeks. The fair on the Vrijdagmarkt in Ghent coincides with the 10-day Gentse Feesten (Ghent Festivities), which are held across the entire inner city around July 21 (the Belgian national holiday).

Another important holiday (which is, however, not an official public holiday) takes place each year on December 6, called Sinterklaasdag in Dutch or la Saint-Nicolas in French (the saint's day of St. Nicholas). This day is a kind of early Christmas. On the evening of December 5, before going to bed, kids put their shoes by the hearth along with some water or wine and a carrot for St. Nicholas's horse or donkey (rather than the reindeer that the youngsters in the United States and Canada expect). Supposedly St. Nicholas arrives at night and descends down the chimney. He takes the food and the water or wine, leaves presents, goes back up the chimney, feeds his horse

Since 1549 (or 1395, according to some) the town of Binche has welcomed the arrival of spring with a carnival. The main attractions are male performers called gilles, whose elaborate attire includes ostrich-feather hats, wax masks, and clogs, which they tap to drive away the spirits of winter. On the carnival's final day, they march through the streets to the rhythm of drums and hand out oranges to the crowd.

or donkey, and continues on his way. He also knows whether kids have been good or bad. Dutch immigrants brought this tradition to the United States, where—of course—St. Nicholas is now known as Santa Claus.

A Brussels landmark that tourists to the city always seek out is a statue that commemorates the supposed heroic act of a small child. The Manneken Pis is a small bronze fountain sculpture of a little boy urinating. The legend is that, when the city was under siege in the fourteenth century, its attackers placed explosive charges within the city walls to destroy them.

A little boy from Brussels who was spying on them rushed out and urinated on the burning fuse, thus saving the city. In any case, it makes a good story, and the city treats the statue with respect—dressing it in various costumes for festivals and other occasions.

The costume-changing is done during ceremonies that are often accompanied by brass-band music. When the fountain is turned on again, the pressure sometimes causes people in the crowd to be sprinkled with water, to everyone's delight. As a result of feminist pressure, the Manneken statue now has a female equivalent, the Jeanneke Pis, a 1987 statue of a small girl similarly occupied on the other side of the Grand-Place. Europe's liberal attitudes toward such works of art are not always deemed so acceptable in the United States. In 2002, a Belgian waffle-maker in Florida set up a replica of the Manneken Pis in front of his waffle stand in the Fashion Square Mall in Orlando. Shocked shoppers made formal complaints, and mall officials banned the display, claiming that it was in violation of the owner's lease.

Sports

Football (or soccer, as it is known in the United States) is undoubtedly the most popular sport in Belgium. The national team and certain clubs in the Belgian football league system, such as Bruges's Club Bruge and Liège's Standard de Liège, have a considerable reputation. A national Belgian football association was founded as long ago as 1895, and the game has a considerable following among members of both the Flemish and the Walloon communities. Much to the dismay of Belgians, the national football team did not qualify for the 2010 World Cup competition.

Other popular Belgian sports include cycling, tennis, swimming, and judo. A Belgian Sportsman of the Year and Sportswoman of the Year are elected annually. The sports already mentioned are usually those in which the winners of these competitions compete, but winners have also been selected from the sports of motor racing and motocross. As we have already seen, Belgium's most successful sportsman ever is the cyclist Eddy Merckx, who was chosen in 2000 as "Sports Figure of the Century."

PUBLIC SAFETY

According to the U.S. State Department, Belgium is a relatively safe country compared with its neighbors. However, other sources dispute this claim. According to Urban Audit, an organization that reports a range of statistics for cities in the EU, in 2001, Brussels had the fourth-highest number of recorded crimes among all European capitals. According to the same source, Brussels had a rate of 10 murders or violent deaths per 100,000 citizens, which was five times higher than in Paris (2 per 100,000). This rate was twice as high as London's, but the overall crime rate was similar to that of Paris. In 2009, Brussels experienced more domestic burglaries than any other European capital, by a rather wide margin. Belgium's second largest city, Antwerp, experienced crime rates about 20 percent below those of Brussels. Charleroi and Liège, industrial cities with high unemployment rates in Wallonia, had more elevated crime rates than the less industrialized cities of Ghent and Bruges in Flanders.

Following a series of shocking murders in recent years, Belgians have become increasingly worried about violent crime—something that was extremely rare not too long ago in this country. Several attacks on armored vans were carried out in the last 20 years, often resulting in the killing of the security agents in charge. However, the most infamous and horrifying crime of recent years is what has become known as the Affaire Dutroux. A series of kidnappings, rapes, and murders—not to mention drug dealing, car theft, and muggings—were carried out by a notorious Belgian criminal named Marc Dutroux. The failure of the Belgian police to act swiftly and effectively, and

This is an aerial view of the White March. An estimated 300,000 people marched in Brussels in October 1996 to express their widespread anger and frustration with the Belgian authorities and slow justice system in the Marc Dutroux case. Dutroux is considered so evil that more than a third of Belgians with the name applied to have their name changed between 1996 and 2004.

the slowness of the judiciary to bring charges against Dutroux, led to widespread anger and discontent among the public. This culminated in a mass protest, known as the White March, in which 300,000 people marched on Brussels in October 1996.

The scandal led to the reorganization of Belgium's law enforcement agencies. Dutroux, an unemployed electrician who lived in Charleroi, had a long criminal history. After being jailed for the rape of five young girls in 1986, he was sentenced to 13½ years in prison. Released after three years, he and an accomplice kidnapped two 8-year-old girls in 1995 and imprisoned and abused them in a basement dungeon in one of his seven houses. Two months later, he kidnapped and imprisoned two more girls, ages 17 and 19, whom he later murdered. From December 1995 to March 1996, he was in custody while police investigated his involvement with stolen luxury cars. Police searched the house looking for evidence in relation to the car theft charges. At the time, the young girls were still alive in the hidden dungeon, but they were not found. Tragically, they starved to death sometime during the following three months, while Dutroux was detained. He also murdered an accomplice and later claimed that he did so because the man had allowed the girls to starve while Dutroux was in police custody.

In May and August 1996, Dutroux separately kidnapped two more teenaged girls, whom he held captive in his dungeon. At this point, a witness remembered part of a license plate that matched Dutroux's. On August 13, 1996, Dutroux and his wife were arrested, but a search of his houses did not turn up anything. Two days later, they both confessed and led police investigators to the dungeon, where the two girls were discovered alive. During his trial (which was delayed for eight years, until 2004), Dutroux claimed that he was part of a Europe-wide prostitution ring. He indicated that his accomplices included Belgian police officers, businessmen, doctors, and even politicians. Nonetheless, he received the maximum sentence of life imprisonment. In 1998, two years after his arrest, a 17-month investigation by a parliamentary commission found that he did not have accomplices in high office, as he continued to claim. The commission did, however, sternly blame the police and judiciary for failing to bring Dutroux to justice earlier and for their corruption, sloppiness, and general incompetence.

Although the public, so many of whom had joined the White March 18 months before, accepted these findings, deep suspicion remained that Dutroux did indeed have friends in high places. There was further public outrage in 1998, when Dutroux overpowered a guard while being taken to a court-house, took his gun, and escaped. Although he was soon recap-tured, the justice minister, the minister of the interior, and the police chief all resigned as a result. The Affaire Dutroux was considered so evil and notorious that more than one-third of Belgians with the quite common last name of Dutroux applied to have their names changed between 1996 and the trial!

In addition to general safety issues, Brussels is believed to serve as a hub for terrorists, as reported by various sources (such as Interpol and local newspapers). In the same urban areas that pose safety problems, there is radicalization and active recruitment by terrorist organizations such as al Qaeda. As stated by Hind Fraihi of the journal *Het Nieuwsblad*, the recruitment is done in mosques (Islamic religious centers), with the actual training done in Afghanistan. Recently, a female suicide bomber in Iraq, Muriel Degauque, became the first Western suicide bomber in modern terrorism. She was not trained in Brussels but in Charleroi, one of the cities with the highest crime rates in the country. The Moroccan Islamic Combatant Group (Groupe Islamique Combattant Marocain, or GICM), which is an ally of al Qaeda, also has links in Bel-gium. There were arrests in Brussels and Antwerp of individu-als connected with GICM following the carnage of the March 2004 train bombings in Madrid, Spain, in which 191 innocent commuters were killed and 2,050 injured.

UNEXPLAINED FLYING OBJECTS

To conclude this chapter, let us look briefly at an intriguing mystery that gripped Belgium during the years 1988 to 1991 and remains unexplained to the present day. All across the country, thousands of people reported sightings of strange black triangular aircraft in the skies. These unidentified flying objects (UFOs) were unlike any known airplanes. These were seen mostly at night, and they often hovered, or moved slowly and silently, at low altitudes. Generally, three bright white lights were said to be fixed at the corners of these thick triangular shapes, and a central red light was often seen shining brightly down from their centers.

Two gendarmes (police officers) in a patrol car, Heinrich Nicholl and Hubert Montigny, spotted just such a huge object in the sky near the city of Eupen (in Liège province) on November 29, 1989. They described it as the size of a football field floating in the air and with strong "headlights" shining down from its three corners. For nearly an hour, they followed it as it hovered over the fields, sometimes bathing the ground below in light. A police dispatcher in Eupen to whom they reported it later saw the same object from his window as it flew over the city. The gendarmes then saw a second similar object appear, before both vanished out of sight.

Six minutes later, two other gendarmes at La Calamine, eight miles (13 kilometers) north of the city, saw another dark triangular craft in the sky. Again, they described it as huge and wondered whether it could be a U.S. military aircraft. This one silently moved low over a church, and the gendarmes watched as a pulsating red light descended from the center of the triangle and flew around before returning to the craft. Then, the three white corner lights seemed to move together and merge into a single bright light. This light flew away at high speed, leaving the sky empty and the two men totally bewildered.

There were reports of similar objects in the skies over Brussels, Liège, Namur, and other Belgian cities. On March 30,

1990, citizens of Ans (a suburb of Liège) saw another unidentified triangular object hovering silently over the city. Local
police officials arrived and reported seeing the object hover
over apartment buildings. Again, one officer reported a glow-
ing red disk of light, which descended from the huge triangle
and darted around several buildings before disappearing. The
larger object eventually took off at high speed.

On several occasions, the Belgium Air Force had scrambled
fighter jets to pursue these objects, but usually without success.
During the Ans sighting, however—during which the objects
also were detected by ground radar systems—two F-16 fighter
planes were sent up. These planes managed to achieve target
lock-on in three of nine attempts during an hour-long pursuit.
Yet, on each occasion, the object would shoot away within sec-
onds at speeds estimated to have exceeded 1,000 miles per hour
(900 knots). Radar recordings from one of the F-16s show the
object flying upward and then descending at a rate of accelera-
tion that would have proved fatal to human pilots.

At a press conference called by the Belgian Air Force, Major
General Wilfried De Brouwer—who was general-aviator of
the air force and the third ranking member of the Belgian
military hierarchy—described the pursuit by the F-16s and
spoke of the thousands of unidentified flying object (UFO)
sightings. He had no explanation for what these unidentified flying objects might have been, other than to say that
the flight characteristics were outside the performance ability
of any known military aircraft. He excluded the possibility
that the objects were U.S. stealth aircraft, saying that the craft
observed could remain stationary at very low altitudes, hardly
moving. Balloons, ultralight aircraft, and unmanned aerial
vehicles (UAVs) were similarly rejected as explanations due
to the highly variable speeds observed. He rejected the sug-
gestion that the radar images were caused by electromagnetic
interference because both the radar of the F-16s and the North
Atlantic Treaty Organization (NATO) ground radar at Glons

had tracked it. Likewise, had any of the observed objects been laser or light projections, they would not have been detectable on radar.

In 1990, General Brouwer admitted that something was going on over Belgium that was "beyond our control." He believed it to be "our job to find where it comes from" and to identify its origins and intentions. Today, however, the sightings remain as great a mystery as they were nearly two decades ago. Since the Belgian sightings, similar craft have been reported over Germany, Britain, Russia, and the United States. There was certainly no proof of their extraterrestrial origin, even though this conclusion was drawn and accepted by many witnesses of these mysterious appearances.

8

Belgium
Looks Ahead

The author has been careful to emphasize the difference between Belgium and what is now increasingly referred to in Europe as "Brussels." The former is the country and its people, and "Brussels" is a term often used for the huge controlling bureaucracy that is the European Union (EU). This powerful entity is not to the liking of all Europeans. Belgium, however, being at its heart, is now virtually impossible to imagine without it. As a result of increased integration within the EU, and its growing membership, what future will there be for Belgium with Brussels as the power capital of Europe?

The EU has grown enormously in recent years. It was created by six founding states in 1957 and now consists of 27 member countries. There have been five enlargements, with the largest occurring in 2004, when 10 states joined. Most recently, on January 1, 2007, Bulgaria and Romania joined the EU. A number of other countries that once formed part of Eastern Europe's Soviet bloc also have applied

Although many EU countries have benefited from a more unified Europe, major challenges still lie ahead. A 2005 CIA report predicted that the EU would break up or Europe would go into economic decline by 2020 due to its aging population and its failing welfare system. The 27 member countries are divided over how best to tackle these issues in the years to come.

for membership. So, too, has Turkey, which is principally an Islamic country and one whose EU membership application is a source of much controversy.

The rush by all of these countries to join the EU is clearly because they all see the enormous economic benefits of membership. Poorer countries, such as Ireland, which joined in 1973, have prospered enormously. Since joining, the difference between what Ireland paid in and what the EU has paid out has been about 34 billion euros (approximately $42 billion). This money was spent on marketing Ireland as the ideal European business location, and on promoting Dublin as the most youthful, vibrant European city. The economic transformation of

Ireland has to be seen to be believed, and many new EU member countries doubtlessly anticipate similar advantages.

However, those European nations with more powerful and established economies, such as France, Germany, and Britain, are aware that, despite increased commerce, it is largely they who are funding such economic revival in other parts of the EU. Anti-EU sentiment has grown in recent years. Several EU countries even have pursued policies aimed at terminating EU membership, or at least at reducing the demands and the intrusive requirements that membership imposes.

In 2005, voters in France and the Netherlands rejected terms of a new EU constitution that was presented to them for ratification. There were similar indications of discontent from voters in other countries, such as Britain, which were also established EU members. When these matters were put to the test in a referendum, those for and against these EU rules were fairly evenly balanced. Some governments, such as that of Britain, held back from offering the electorate a referendum on the EU despite having made election pledges to do so. If the European Union did start to fragment, it is clear that this would have a marked effect on the future of Belgium.

Without the presence of the EU in Brussels, one can only speculate about whether the country of Belgium itself would separate into independent Flemish-speaking and French-speaking states. There is indeed a strong Flemish nationalist movement in Belgium that has an independent Flanders as its aim. Vlaams Belang (VB; in English, Flemish Interest) is the political party that supports Flemish independence and the placement of strict limits on non-European and non-Christian immigration. This party insists that immigrants need to adopt and adapt to Western culture. VB rejects multiculturalism, although it accepts a multiethnic society that would exclude Islam. Although the party describes its current policies as those of a traditional conservative party, many observers describe them as far right, and some members have been accused of being Nazi sympathizers. In any case,

In September 2006, the French-speaking Belgian Parliament introduced a bill limiting the number of foreign students, mainly French, to 30 percent. The European Commission has threatened to take legal action against Belgium (and Austria for similar legislation) for restricting foreign students' access to national higher education institutions within member-states. Pictured here are students protesting the bill.

VB showed strong results in the 2006 municipal elections in Flanders, apart from Antwerp. Like the CD&V party, it enjoyed a massive increase of votes, nearly doubling the number of VB council members from 439 to about 800.

One may well ask: Is the division of Belgium into separate independent states a real possibility sometime in the near future? Despite those who would wish for such a division, there are many Belgians who strongly oppose anything other than national unity. In 1993, Belgium's King Baudouin died after reigning for 42 years. His death was unexpected and sent much of Belgium into a period of deep mourning. He was succeeded by his younger brother, who became King Albert II.

After his father, Leopold III, abdicated in 1951, Baudouin brought stability (although not harmony) to a country gripped by the struggle between Dutch-speaking Flanders and French-speaking Wallonia. At the time of Baudouin's death, Belgium had begun to implement a far-reaching federalization that made the maintenance of Belgian unity questionable. The wave of mourning that marked the passing of Baudouin brought Flemings and Walloons together in support of the monarchy. There certainly was no support for a designated deputy who shouted in favor of a European republic before Albert took his oath. This call for a republic during the royal investiture is a Belgian tradition. Some republicans had anticipated that, early in the new millennium, there would be a rush to full separation into independent states. It became evident, however, that the Belgians were committed to the dynasty and preservation of the country.

The general election of 2007, however, has caused this vexing problem of national fragmentation to arise once again. Six months after the election, Yves Leterme, a Flemish Christian Democrat whose party had triumphed in June, abandoned his second attempt to form an administration, and King Albert accepted his request to be relieved of the coalition-forming task. Leterme is, however, a controversial figure who once branded Belgium as an accident of history and joked that the country's French speakers were too stupid to learn Dutch. In 2010, Flemish and Walloon politicians still were hotly debating Belgium's future. They were unable to reach a compromise over whether the country should be split into an independent Flanders and an independent Wallonia. Even so, this lack of national government and the failure of Flemish and Walloon politicians to reach a compromise do indeed raise the question of whether the country should be split into an independent Flanders and an independent Wallonia. If this were to happen, Brussels would become a kind of Washington, D.C., for the European Union, and Belgium as such would cease to exist. Is such a scenario possible? We can only wait and see.

Physical Geography

Location	Western Europe; bordering the North Sea, the Netherlands, Germany, Luxembourg, and France
Area	Total: 11,787 square miles (30,528 square kilometers), about the size of Maryland; land: 18,813 square miles (30,278 square kilometers); water: 155 square miles (250 square kilometers)
Boundaries	Border countries: France, 385 miles (620 kilometers); Germany, 103 miles (167 kilometers); Luxembourg, 91.9 (148 kilometers); and the Netherlands, 279.6 miles (450 kilometers)
Coastline	41 miles (66.5 kilometers), facing upon the Strait of Dover
Climate	Temperate; mild winters, cool summers; rainy, humid, cloudy
Terrain	Flat coastal plains in northwest; central rolling hills; fairly rugged hills and mountains of the Ardennes in southeast
Elevation Extremes	Lowest point, North Sea (sea level); highest point, Signal de Botrange, 2,277 feet (694 meters)
Land Use	Arable land, 27.42%; permanent crops, 0.69%; other, 71.89% Note: includes Luxembourg (2005)
Irrigated Land	248 square miles (400 square kilometers) (2003)
Natural Hazards	Flooding is a threat along rivers and in areas of reclaimed coastal land protected from the sea by concrete dikes
Natural Resources	Construction materials, silica sand, carbonates
Environmental Issues	Intense pressures from human activities: urbanization, dense transportation network, industry, extensive animal breeding and crop cultivation; air and water pollution also have repercussions for neighboring countries; uncertainties regarding federal and regional responsibilities (now resolved) have slowed progress in tackling environmental challenges

People

Population	10,423,493 (July 2010 est.)
Population Density	884 people per square mile (342 per square kilometer)
Population Growth Rate	0.08% per year (2010 est.)

Net Migration Rate	1.22 migrant(s)/1,000 population (2010 est.)
Total Fertility Rate	1.65 children born per woman (2010 est.)
Birth Rate	10.1 births/1,000 population (2010 est.)
Death Rate	10.5 deaths/1,000 population (2010 est.)
Life Expectancy at Birth	Total population: 79.4 years; male, 76.2 years; female, 82.7 years (2010 est.)
Median Age	Total: 42 years; male, 41 years; female, 43 years (2010 est.)
Ethnic Groups	Fleming, 58%; Walloon, 31%; mixed or other, 11%
Religion	Roman Catholic, 75%; other, (includes Protestant), 25%
Language	Dutch (official), 60%; French (official), 40%; German (official), less than 1%
Literacy	(Age 15 and over can read and write) Total population: 99% (99%, male; 99%, female) (2003)

Economy

Currency	Euro
GDP Purchasing Power Parity (PPP)	$381 billion (2009 est.)
GDP Per Capita	$36,600 (2009 est.)
Labor Force	5 million (2009 est.)
Unemployment Rate	8.3% (2009 est.)
Labor Force by Occupation	Services, 73.7%; industry, 25%; agriculture, 2% (2007 est.)
Agricultural Products	Sugar beets, fresh vegetables, fruits, grain, tobacco; beef, veal, pork, milk
Industries	Engineering and metal products, motor vehicle assembly, transportation equipment, scientific instruments, processed food and beverages, chemicals, basic metals, textiles, glass, petroleum
Exports	$296 billion f.o.b. (2009 est.)
Imports	$315 billion f.o.b. (2009 est.)
Leading Trade Partners	Exports: Germany, 19.8%; France, 17.4%; Netherlands, 19.4%; U.K., 7.2%; U.S., 4.8%; Italy, 4.7% (2008). Imports: Netherlands, 19.4%; Germany, 17.2%; France, 11.1%; U.K., 5.7%; U.S., 5.5%; China, 4.1% (2008)
Export Commodities	Machinery and equipment, chemicals, diamonds, metals and metal products, foodstuffs

Import Commodities	Machinery and equipment, chemicals, diamonds, pharmaceuticals, foodstuffs, transportation equipment, oil products
Transportation	Roadways: 94,607 miles (152,256 kilometers); 73,992 miles (119,079 kilometers) are paved; Railways: 2,009 miles (3,233 kilometers): Airports: 43; 27 with paved runways; Waterways: 1,269 miles (2,043 kilometers)

Government

Country Name	Conventional long form: Kingdom of Belgium; Conventional short form: Belgium: Local long form: Royaume de Belgique/Koninkrijk Belgie; Local short form: Belgique/Belgie
Capital City	Brussels
Type of Government	Federal parliamentary democracy under a constitutional monarchy
Independence	October 4, 1830 (a provisional government declared independence from the Netherlands); July 21, 1831 (King Leopold I ascended to the throne)
Administrative Divisions	10 provinces and 3 regions

NOTE: As a result of the 1993 constitutional revision that furthered devolution into a federal state, there are now three levels of government (federal, regional, and linguistic community) with complex divisions of responsibilities.

Communications

TV Stations	25
Radio Stations	86 (AM: 7, FM: 79) (1998)
Phones	16.279 million (including 11.822 million cell phones)
Internet Users	7.29 million (2008)

NOTE: All data, unless otherwise indicated, are based on 2010 figures. These and other statistical data can be obtained and updated on an annual basis using the *CIA- The World Factbook* (annual updates).

800,000 B.C.	Primitive Stone Age implements indicate region's inhabitation (approximate date).
350,000 to 40,000 B.C.	Neanderthal man lives on the banks of the River Meuse and was eventually supplanted by *Homo sapiens*.
3000–1500 B.C.	Neolithic dolmens and passage graves are built in the Liège region.
c. 75 B.C.	Roman legions subdue the Celtic Belgae tribes in a region they call Gallia Belgica.
A.D. 400	Gallia Belgica is invaded by the Germanic tribes of the Franks.
768–814	Charlemagne reigns as king of the Franks; capital is at Aachen.
c. 1000–1200	Ghent, then known as Gaunt, flourishes as the second-largest city in Europe.
1363–1477	Low Countries become part of the domain of the French Dukes of Burgundy and so are embroiled in the Hundred Years War (1337–1453) between France and England.
1477	Charles the Bold is killed at the Battle of Nancy; domain of the Low Countries passes to the Habsburgs, Austrian rulers of the Holy Roman Empire.
1504–1700	The land that is today's Belgium becomes the Spanish Netherlands.
1579	The Union of Utrecht is proclaimed; under William I of Orange, the Northern provinces secede and the Dutch revolt against Spain continues throughout the Eighty Years War, until 1648.
1701–1714	War of the Spanish Succession is fought; the battles of Ramillies, Oudenarde, and Malplaquet take place.
1748	Austrian rule is restored; under Empress Maria Theresa, there is new prosperity.
1794	The armies of revolutionary France defeat the Austrians and annex what is now Belgium.
1814–1815	The Congress of Vienna agrees to unify the Low Countries as the United Kingdom of the Netherlands (before the brief return to power from exile by Napoleon).

1815	The Battle of Waterloo is fought; the final defeat of French emperor Napoleon's army by the British and Dutch/Belgian forces, together with their Prussian allies, takes place.
1830	The Belgian Revolution establishes an independent, neutral, and Catholic Belgium.
1831	Leopold of Saxe-Coburg is chosen as king of the new country and is enthroned.
1885	King Leopold II acquires the Congo Free State, which becomes his private domain.
1908	Belgium takes control of the Belgian Congo from King Leopold II.
1914	Germany invades Belgium after demand of passage for its troops is refused.
1914–1918	World War I battles are fought across Belgium and Northern France.
1927	George Lemaître proposes the big bang theory of the creation of the universe.
1930	The Belgian government recognizes Dutch as the only official language of Flanders; Dutch-speaking and French-speaking areas of administration are defined.
1940–1944	World War II occupation of Belgium by Nazi Germany occurs.
1944	Ardennes Offensive: The Battle of the Bulge between the U.S. Army and German troops is fought until 1945.
1949	The United States, Belgium, and the other European allies sign the North Atlantic Treaty.
1951	King Leopold III abdicates in favor of his son King Baudouin I.
1957	The Treaty of Rome is signed; the European Economic Community (EEC) is formed, a precursor to the European Union (EU).
1960	The Belgian Congo is granted independence; Ruanda-Urundi gains independence in 1962.
1967	The North Atlantic Treaty Organization (NATO) headquarters and Supreme Headquarters Allied Powers Europe (SHAPE) are relocated to Belgium.

1992–1993	The Treaty of Maastricht leads to the creation of the EU, replacing the earlier EEC and specifying protocols for European monetary and political union.
1993	Constitutional amendments and new federalization measures are introduced in the Belgian parliament; Albert II succeeds Baudouin as king of the Belgians.
1999–2007	Guy Verhofstadt of the Vlaamse Liberalen en Democraten (VLD) party leads two consecutive Purple Coalition governments of Liberals and Socialists.
2002	The Belgian franc is replaced by the euro, the official EU standard unit of currency.
2003	Legislation approved to close Belgium's seven nuclear reactors by 2025 and ban the building of new nuclear facilities.
2007	Prime Minister Guy Verhofstadt resigns after his ruling coalition suffers election losses, resulting in a 100 day power vacuum during which Belgium was without a government. In December, Verhofstadt reappointed to head interim government.
2008	Yves Leterme sworn in as new head of government, but four months later offers to resign due to inability to reach a power-sharing arrangement between Flemish (Dutch speaking) and Walloon (French speaking) regions of the country. King Albert II refuses to accept resignation. Country experiences financial crisis and scandal resulting in resignation of Prime Minister Yves Leterme
2009	Christian Democrat Herman Van Rompuy becomes prime minister, but steps down to become President of the European Council. He is replaced by Yves Leterme.
2010	Political turbulence continues including a collapse of the government. The separatist New Flemish Alliance becomes the largest political party and the French Socialist Party gains power in Wallonia.

The World Factbook 2009. Washington, D.C.: Central Intelligence Agency, 2009. Available online at https://www.cia.gov/library/publications/the-world-factbook/.

"Internet Usage in Europe." Internet World Stats. Available online at http://www.internetworldstats.com/stats4.htm.

"UFO in Eupen, Belgium." Short French-language video. Available online at http://www.youtube.com/watch?v=tIGXdv-Chjo&mode=related&search=.

Wikipedia-The Free Online Encyclopedia. Available online at http://en.wikipedia.org/wiki/Main_Page.

Wright, John W., ed. *The New York Times Almanac.* New York: Penguin, 2007.

Further Reading

Cammaerts, Emile. *A History of Belgium from The Roman Invasion to the Present Day.* New York: D. Appleton and Co., 1921.

de Kavanagh Boulger, and Demetrius Charles. *Belgium of the Belgians.* New York: C. Scribner's Sons, 1918.

————. *The History of Belgium: Part 1—Caesar to Waterloo.* London: Adamant Media Corporation, 2005 (reprint of 1902 original).

————. *The History of Belgium: Part 2—1815–1865. Waterloo to the Death of Leopold I.* London: Adamant Media Corporation, 2005 (reprint of the 1909 original).

Goscinny, Rene, and Albert Uderzo. *Asterix in Belgium.* London: Orion, 2005.

Logan, Leanne, and Geert Cole. *Lonely Planet Belgium & Luxembourg.* London and Oakland, CA: Lonely Planet Publications, 2007.

McDonald, George. *Frommer's Belgium, Holland, and Luxembourg.* Hoboken, NJ: Wiley Publications, Inc., 2005.

Web Sites

Belgian Culture
http://pespmcl.vub.ac.be/BELGCUL.html

CIA World Factbook—Belgium
https://www.cia.gov/library/publications/the-world-factbook/print/be.html

Introduction to Belgium
http://www.visitbelgium.com

Index

Index

About the Contributors

GEORGE WINGFIELD is a graduate of Trinity College in Dublin, Ireland, where he earned both a B.A. and an M.A. in natural sciences. He has worked as an astronomer at the Royal Greenwich Observatory and as an engineer and consultant for IBM. He has contributed to a number of books on the crop-circle phenomenon in Britain and, in 1992, presented a lecture on the topic at the Smithsonian Institution and appeared on *Larry King Live*. In 2007, he published *Prehistoric Sacred Sites of Wessex* and *Glastonbury Isle of Avalon*. He currently leads tours of ancient and sacred sites in England, Scotland, and Ireland.

CHARLES F. "FRITZ" GRITZNER is Distinguished Professor Emeritus of Geography at South Dakota State University in Brookings. In 2010, he retired after a 50-year career of college teaching. He enjoys travel, writing, and sharing his love for and knowledge of geography with readers. Gritzner has contributed to Chelsea House's MODERN WORLD NATIONS, MAJOR WORLD CULTURES, EXTREME ENVIRONMENTS, and GLOBAL CONNECTIONS series. He has served as both President and Executive Director of the National Council for Geographic Education (NCGE) and has received the Council's highest honor, the George J. Miller Award for Distinguished Service to Geographic Education, as well as numerous other national teaching, service, and research recognitions from the NCGE, the Association of American Geographers, and other organizations. Gritzner lives in South Dakota with his wife, Yvonne, and their "family" of two Italian Greyhounds.